Selling cars will be the highest paying,
easiest work you'll ever do...or selling cars will be
one of the lowest paying, hardest jobs you'll ever have!

The Difference Will Be Goal Setting

You don't even need rocket science to figure out why.
When you wing it every day, you've set yourself up for failure.
With clear goals and a plan, you've set yourself up for success.

MANAGE YOUR
CAREER IN SALES

GOAL SETTING
FOR SALESPEOPLE

Having a clear goal, and a daily plan of action to grow and improve, sure beats just hoping you sell something while you put in double shifts most days just to make a living.

> *I know it's true because*
> *I've been there – done that.*

I spent my first five years as an 8-car guy and it was a struggle every month. But once I learned how to use goal setting to control my career, my life has never been the same.

Follow the guidelines I'll give you in this book, and I can promise you'll increase your sales and income right now – and if you keep doing what I'll cover, you will continue to improve and grow in sales and in every area of your life.

JOE VERDE

Joe Verde Sales & Management Training, Inc.

Books by Joe Verde

How To Sell A Car And Close The Sale Today

38 Hot Tips On Selling More Cars In Today's Market

A Dealer's Guide To Recovery And Growth In Today's Market

Earn Over $100,000 Selling Cars – Every Year

MANAGE YOUR
CAREER IN SALES

GOAL SETTING
FOR SALESPEOPLE

Copyright © 2013

by Joe Verde

ISBN#: 978-1-4675-5827-3

2nd Edition Printed in the United States of America

joeverde.com • (800) 445-6217 • (949) 489-3780

In Dedication To Zig Ziglar...

I regularly mention Zig Ziglar in my books, our workshops and online on JVTN®, regarding the great impact he had on me and my career.

We were recording our Goal Setting Course for JVTN® last week, and had just talked about Mr. Ziglar in one of the chapters. We learned the next day, that he had passed away.

Zig Ziglar changed so many lives with his many books, tapes, and seminars, and he helped so many people reach potential they didn't even know they had.

My favorite book has always been Zig Ziglar's book, "See You At The Top". In that one book, he changed my life.

Thank you, Mr. Ziglar, for everything you did for all of us.

A loyal and devoted fan, always...

Joe Verde

"You were born to win, but to be a winner, you must plan to win, prepare to win, and expect to win."

– Zig Ziglar

"Most people spend their lives waiting for something good to happen. Only a few ever realize life is a do-it-yourself project."

– Joe Verde

TABLE OF CONTENTS

A Note From Joe's General Manager

The question most people have right now is...

"Why should I listen to Joe Verde about how to set goals?"

It's a great question, and the answer is easy...

Joe grew up on a small farm in Texas, just outside a town of 900 people. If you've been to any of his workshops or read his other books, you know he always laughs about how he 'escaped' the farm by joining the Army, as soon as he turned 18.

He spent 7 years in the Army, 5 of those as a helicopter mechanic, and for 26 months, including his 20th and 21st birthday, he was in Vietnam. He served there as a CH-47 Helicopter Crew Chief, Flight Engineer, Door Gunner, Tech Inspector and Platoon Sergeant.

He flew during some of the worst times during the Vietnam War, and earned several rows of medals and awards for his service. As a maintenance platoon leader, when he was just 20 years old, his men kept more helicopters flying missions than any other platoon in the entire Battalion. Because of the exceptional performance of his team, just two months after his 21st birthday, Joe was the youngest person ever promoted to the rank of E-6 in his Battalion.

After Joe got out of the Army, he started selling cars in Anaheim, California. Like 90% of the salespeople with no training, for 5 years he was stuck in that 8-car per month rut he talks about in class.

He stopped selling cars after 5 years and opened an accessory business working with auto dealers. That's when he finally got his training on how to sell – through dozens of books and audio courses. Joe credits Zig Ziglar with waking him up about goal setting and the other success skills it takes to become a high achiever, and to keep growing year after year.

After a couple of years, Joe started selling cars again and immediately went from his old school 8-unit level to selling 38 units a month overnight – and made more money selling cars in his first 7 months back in the business, than he had made in his first 5 years combined.

*Listen to Joe – so you can learn from someone
who has actually done what they're telling you to do.*

But that isn't all. In 1985, Joe founded Joe Verde Sales and
Management Training, Inc. to share what he'd learned with dealers,
managers and salespeople, and almost immediately he became the
#1 Sales Trainer in the car business. At his first presentation at the
National Automobile Dealers Convention, his workshops were
beyond sold out – we were told that his attendance was the highest
they'd ever recorded.

Joe changes people's lives in his classes and on JVTN® by teaching
you how to do the same things that changed his own life. No matter
what level you're at in sales, management, or as a dealer, Joe can
teach you how to move from wherever you are now up to your next
level, and he'll show you how to keep having record years, every year,
just like he has continued to do throughout his life.

Joe exemplifies true professionalism, and through his leadership,
our company has had 24 record years in our 27 years in business,
with an average growth rate per year of over 50%.

Joe teaches you exactly what he does to continually set records.

Joe was the first automotive trainer to offer online training
worldwide to salespeople and managers, so they could develop
their skills and continue their education at home or work. Over
8,000,000 (8 million) chapters of his online training courses on
JVTN® have been taken by dealers, managers and salespeople. This
year, close to 2 million more training chapters will be taken online.

Recovery & Growth after the recession...

Joe Verde also led the charge in the car business to help as many
dealers as possible recover, stabilize and grow during and after the
recession. His book, "A Dealer's Guide To Recovery & Growth,"
is currently in its 6th printing, and has helped thousands of dealers
survive and thrive again, after the worst recession in our industry.

*More people have used Joe's training to improve
than all other automotive trainers combined.*

The Undisputed Leader In Training!

Our company holds sales and management training workshops for the automobile business across North America. We have held thousands of our own workshops, plus hundreds of special events for state, local and other associations and for dealer groups and automobile manufacturers around the world.

Joe Verde Sales & Management Training, Inc., is by far the most recognized and most recommended automotive sales, management and leadership training company in the world, and Joe has 'been there – done that' on every topic he teaches. He walks the walk and will show you how to become the number one person in any position you hold, too.

Joe's methods are clear, concise, and proven, which is so important to you because you can actually learn and do everything Joe teaches. Follow Joe's methods in his workshops and on JVTN® (Joe Verde's Training Network®) – and you will improve your selling skills. Follow his guidelines in this book on how to set and reach your goals – and you will succeed beyond your wildest dreams at everything you choose to do.

It's simple – listen to Joe, because his training works!

Kathleen Rittmaster

General Manager

Joe Verde Sales & Management Training, Inc.

WHAT'S A GOAL ...?

"A DREAM WITH A DEADLINE."

– Napoleon Hill

Why Read A Book On Goal Setting?

In my first 5 years selling cars, every day was almost as long as most of my days were in Vietnam. Over there, we worked from 5 or so in the morning to get our helicopters ready to fly, then we'd fly all day and come back when it got dark. Then we'd work as long as it took until they were ready to fly again tomorrow. The next day was just like the last one – *same stuff, different day.*

> I just repeated that same day in Vietnam
> over and over again, 809 times in a row.

I got out of the Army, was a bartender for a year, and finally started selling cars in California in one of those hard T.O. stores – and just like hard workers everywhere with good intentions, I gave selling cars my very best shot.

Our schedule said we'd either have Tuesday or Thursday off each week, and once a month we'd get a weekend. In real life, almost all of us worked bell-to-bell instead of the posted morning and afternoon shifts, and we came in on almost every day off.

We really didn't have a choice about spending so much of our time working in the dealership every day, because we couldn't sell – *we just didn't know how.* Most of us had families to feed and I had all the normal family bills, too, so I needed to make a sale, no matter how long I had to work.

I was definitely making more than the Army paid back then, but my average month was about $1,500 and my best year was $23,000. So five years into selling cars I was just fed up with long hours, no days off, and the low pay that came with only about 8 deliveries each month. Sure, I thought I *sold* more than 8, but when you deliver anybody with a heartbeat, tons of deals come back – along with all of those charge-backs on my commissions.

I wanted out of selling cars, and I'd gotten friendly with the guy who did our pinstriping at the dealership, so I talked him into teaching me how to do what he did. He agreed, and I'm pretty sure it was because I offered to work for him free for a month as a trade.

Goal Setting

Have you ever been in a bookstore?

I hadn't, but now I needed to learn how to run a business! I was 32, and I had actually done my best to avoid bookstores. Bookstores back then didn't have a coffee shop inside to lure us in, like they have now. They just had books, and I wasn't much into reading.

Because I was opening my first business though, I knew I needed a book on accounting, so I could keep up with what I was doing. I don't know if you've ever been in a bookstore, but I was shocked to find that they had hundreds of books on how to sell, close, overcome objections, follow-up, prospect, use the phones, control your success, run a business – and how to set goals.

I walked out that day with an armload of books. The only problem was that none of them were exactly on how to set specific sales goals for my business (or on how to sell cars). They were all on *generic* goal setting and on selling other stuff like insurance or real estate.

When I was 32, I had less than $500 to my name!
But then two things happened after I started to learn more...

First ... for the next 2 years that I had my accessory business, I spent every free minute reading books, writing my notes, and converting what I was learning about selling houses, insurance, and pots and pans into *scripts* (the words) I could use to sell my products and to sell cars.

I was shocked at the difference between my selling skills from the past, and how easy selling really could be. Starting out with just a few hundred dollars and a $500 credit limit on a charge card, within months, I had 3 trucks servicing accounts. Within a year, I'd opened a retail shop and in two years, I was one of the top 5 companies in that business in Los Angeles and Orange County.

I had already learned how to work hard, and now that I was learning how to sell the right way, sales were great, I was making money, life was good and everything kept getting better.

Second ... and even more important...
I learned how to become successful by learning how
to use goal setting to consistently and continually improve.

*Doesn't just 'selling more' automatically
mean you are more successful?*

Kind of – and it definitely means you'll make more money than you
did before. But we all know too many people who can sell more, but
never really get past 'go' in life, much less improve year after year.

When I learned how to sell, I also learned that everything about
selling is process driven. So I created processes I could follow in
every area – selling on the lot, closing the sale, negotiating, follow up,
prospecting, phones and more. I followed those processes with every
customer and when I started selling cars again, I made more money
my first 7 months back than I did my first 5 years selling combined.

You really should read my books (most are free), attend our
workshops and train online daily on JVTN®. Why? Because the
things you and I were taught about selling will keep you trapped in
that 8-car body too many of you are stuck in right now. You have to
learn more so you can *escape* being average, and I'll show you how.

Goal Setting Is The Secret To Your Success.

Those first books I read were by authors most people reading this have
never even heard of: Napoleon Hill, J. Douglas Edwards, Zig Ziglar,
Art Linkletter, Andrew Carnegie, W. Clement Stone, Ben Franklin,
Plato, Socrates and dozens of others.

These men reached the highest levels of success, and even though
they may have said it differently, each of them taught *the same
exact common sense approach to selling and success*. Ben Franklin
talked about feature, advantage and benefit selling in the 1700s.
Socrates talked about how to control the conversation back in
400 BC and he also said, "Be as you wish to seem," (aka: do what
it takes to succeed). Carnegie said, "People who are unable to
motivate themselves must be content with mediocrity, no matter
how impressive their other talents."

Zig Ziglar was one of the most influential for me. His was one of the
first books I read and he just *rang my bell* on almost everything he
talked about. He made me understand the true power of goal setting,
and *becoming a goal setter literally changed my life.*

From my background, I have always been able to work longer and harder than most people. Living on a farm is an every day job; before school, after school, and during summers while everybody else has fun. You have no choice. Vietnam was the same thing. You had no choice – long hard days, one right after the other.

What I learned from Ziglar and the others is that no matter how hard you work, only a very small percentage of people ever make it to the top. 97% miss out on the real success they could have because *they lack clear goals*. Or as W. Clement Stone would say, they lack a 'definiteness of purpose' (aka: no clear goals).

Is it goal setting – or is it magic?

Goal setting is the best kept secret in the world and it's the closest thing to real magic there could be. It's simple, and it's powerful. You figure out what you want, then write a very detailed plan on how you'll get it, and then presto – if you just follow your plan, 94% of the time you get whatever it was you wanted.

I honestly never thought about setting a goal until I learned from all of those great leaders in sales, business and success. I only had one goal on the farm – escape. I didn't set a goal to be promoted when I was in the Army, I just worked hard. And I certainly had no goals my first time in the car business.

I can tell you that those guys who wrote all those great books were not the equivalent of an 8-car guy. They were mega-rich in the old days and they built industries and empires.

I learned from the most successful people that continuous success in sales, in management, as a business owner, or in any other profession requires four things:

- The skills to do the job
- Clear goals with clear action plans
- A burning desire to succeed
- The discipline to follow your plan

Of course other things are important.

Sure, having a great attitude, a ton of product knowledge, being a team player, and all of those other things that affect success are important, too. But if you lack the skills, if you don't have clear goals and clear plans, if you don't want success badly enough or if you don't have the consistent discipline it takes to follow your plan, you will most likely just become a very positive *average* team player wherever you work.

Zig Ziglar and those other business leaders taught me the skills I'd need to succeed in sales, in business and in life. They also taught me how to set goals correctly (which I'll cover in here) and if you follow these steps you, too, can reach your next level of success.

After reading their books, I also developed the first *burning desire* to succeed I'd ever experienced. For the first time in my life I felt prepared, because I had developed my *skills*, I had clear *goals* and I now had that unwavering *desire* to succeed. And all of my farming days and my time in Vietnam finally paid off big time – because they gave me the *work ethic* and *discipline* it takes to make it happen.

Success is a Journey – not a Destination.

I think the most important thing to remember is that success isn't just the bulls-eye you aim for one time. Success is a constantly forward moving target, and that's why having daily, monthly, yearly and lifetime goals is critical.

The old adage, *you either have what it takes or you don't,* just isn't true. It doesn't matter whether you're young or old, or new or have been selling cars for 30 years. How many (or how few) units you sell your first 60 or 90 days, or first 30 years has almost no impact on how successful you'll become tomorrow, if you just start learning more today about selling – and if you'll learn to set goals to improve.

When you're learning to sell and learning to become successful, it helps to remember you don't have to make giant leaps...

The secret to success is to just keep moving forward!

If you're ready – let's talk about your career!

CHAPTER 1

ARE YOU READY!

The very best way for you to get started on your road to more success in sales, is to ask yourself if you're actually ready. Seriously, think about the question and be honest with yourself, because being ready is your first step.

> Of course you just said,
> *"Sure, I'm ready – show me how."*

The words – *sure, I'm ready* – are correct, but they're most likely just a reflex answer to a question you know you should say *yes* to. It may not be the answer from your heart – where real success has to start.

A reflex answer won't get you to your next level, so stay on this page and think about how far you've come in life up to now, and how much further you really do want to go. When you're ready to start controlling your career in sales and your life, turn the page.

Do you really want to grow – and how badly?

I understand that it's hard to answer these questions because you're not sure what we'll cover. Here's the short version – we are going to cover how you can *sell more, earn more, be more and do more* than you ever thought you would or could. Based on that...

* Are you ready to move to your next level in sales and income, no matter how well you're doing, or think you're doing right now?

* Are you ready to take a tough, honest look at your production, your income and your daily activities so you can grow?

* Are you ready to take a real hard look at your skill level, your work habits, your success attitude and the type of customers you've been choosing to work with in sales?

* Are you ready to make a personal, unwavering commitment to do whatever it takes every day to start, and then keep improving yourself and your levels in sales and success?

* Are you ready to make the trade-offs and make the changes all high achievers agree have to be made to grow and keep growing?

* Are you ready to start really enjoying selling at a professional level and to start earning 2 or 3 or 10 times what you're earning now for you and for your family?

You really do need to honestly think about how far you want to take your success. Why? Because you have no limits on the number of cars you can sell, the amount of money you can earn in sales, or the goals you can achieve.

I know from personal experience that when you can finally answer all of these questions from your heart with an absolutely honest '*Yes*', and then make the real commitment to change, that you can do anything you want to do.

If you're like I was, you'll also find that when you can truly answer '*Yes*', you'll feel an immediate release from everything that's been holding you back – and you'll enthusiastically start your new journey.

Congratulations on taking this first step,
it will change your life!

Turning your wishes and dreams into reality.

If you're like most people, you spend a little, or a lot of time each day *daydreaming*. We all daydream about things (mostly fun things) that we wish we had, but we don't. Things we wish we'd done, but didn't. That's what daydreaming is about. We don't daydream about things we have, we think about things we want.

Remember all the times you've said, "I wish." Do you remember that really good paycheck you got that time – didn't it feel great? Didn't you *wish* you could get one of those every month or every two weeks? I'm guessing your family would also *wish* you got one of those big paychecks more often too, huh?

Wishing is something we learn to do as kids.
We *wish* on stars – we pull the *wish*bone – we do *wish*ful thinking, we toss money into the *wish*ing well – we blow out candles and make a *wish* – we *wish* we'd win the lottery – we *wish* we could sell more – we *wish* we made more money. And how about the pot of gold at the end of the rainbow, don't we *wish* for that, too?

Did you know there really is a secret to getting everything you could possibly wish for? There actually is a way to turn your *wishes* and *dreams* into the real thing. That means you really can go after the *proverbial* pot of gold at the end of the rainbow *and get it.*

Did you notice that word *secret* in the paragraph above? That wasn't just a trick word to get your attention. Setting goals is the most important thing you'll ever learn how to do in life – but the trick is learning how to do it right.

Knowing how to set goals correctly is the secret.

If you'll spend the time it takes to read this book with an open mind and accept some new information, I'll share the secrets of turning your dreams and wishes into real things that you can touch and feel and even deposit in the bank.

If you're really ready to grow and improve,
let's get to work on the first day of the rest of your life.

Setting goals requires an imagination.

Did you know that by the time we're 7 or 8 years old,

we've already lost most of our imagination?

"Our 6 salespeople average 115.5 units every month."

"Joe, thanks to your virtual training on JVTN®, in just 6 months, all 6 of our salespeople have improved by over 5 units per month. They each have a rolling 90-day current average of more than 15 units per salesperson.

Daily training on JVTN® helps our guys stay sharp with their closing skills, and shows them how to present and demonstrate the vehicle that fits closest to their customer's wants and needs.

Now our 90-day average is 115.5 units per month with just 6 salespeople. Thanks, again!" – John, GM, Chrysler Jeep, Indiana

CHAPTER 2

THE FACTS ABOUT
GOAL SETTING & GOAL SETTERS

Before most people are willing to make a change or try something different, they want to know, "What's In It For Me?" and who could blame them.

We reference that important question as "WIIFM" and talk about it as being the only station most of us tune in to – especially when it comes to change.

Let's take a look at the facts about goal setting, who the goal setters are, what they do, and what the benefits are to *you* of becoming a goal setter right away.

If you haven't already – grab a pen, paper and a highlighter and let's talk about what's in it for *you* to start setting clear goals in sales and in your life.

The Facts About Success & Goal Setting

1. As incredible as it sounds, the average person spends more time *planning just one vacation* than they'll spend on improving their work skills or planning for their retirement.

 Think about the planning involved for your first trip to Hawaii with your family. You want beach time, tourist time, you'd like to go horseback riding and you all love hiking.

Let's look at the planning for that simple one week trip...

*   When are you going? You'll definitely need to decide on that so you can book flights, hotel, rental cars, and any tours. Better put in for those days off quick, before someone else does.

*   Pick an island. Do some online research to learn more about each island and the differences. Ask around and find someone who's been – what they liked best, is it easy to get around, what is there to do, where did they stay? How much did it cost?

*   Horseback riding. Better check online to make sure you can rent a horse on that island – where's the stable? Do you need reservations ahead of time? Will you need any special gear?

*   Hiking. How about a day trip? Where can you go, do they have guides, how much will it cost? Better do more research.

*   Beach. What about beach time for the kids? Where would you go? What about that submarine ride you heard about?

*   Find a hotel. On the beach? What price range? Do you want a view? Do they have a fridge and microwave in the room? Any fun things right at the hotel? Any grocery stores close by?

*   Packing. What clothes will you take? Backpacks? How many pairs of shorts? Should you pack a lot of clothes or do the laundry there? Need hats, caps, sunscreen, hair dryer, camera, phones, chargers, cash, ATM card, etc.?

*   Airline tickets. Shop for airfare, pick airlines, pick flights, have alternates, just in case. Want to get there early in the day?

Wow – who would have thought there would be so much to research and plan, just to take a one week vacation to Hawaii. In fact, if this is your first trip there, this could take weeks of research and planning.

Sure, it takes a lot of planning just to take a vacation, and most people wouldn't consider just jumping in the car, heading to the airport, hoping there's a flight, picking an island based on flights with empty seats, and hope there's a hotel room when they get there.

But isn't that what salespeople do every day? Jump in the car and hope for a ton of floor traffic today, hope they'll get a good 'up', hope they're there to buy, hope they can find a car in stock, hope they can sell it, hope the customer can get bought, and hope they have a good month.

Hope is not a strategy!

If you'll spend as much time going over your 5-year sales and lifetime goals as you'd spend planning just one vacation, you'll be guaranteed more great days, great months, great years, and a very successful career (plus a lot more fun vacations).

2. Average U.S. Incomes. These change yearly, but not by much. These are the rounded off break points based on "tax returns by *adjusted gross income*". That means total incomes at the top levels were actually much higher. (U.S. federal income tax data can be found at www.taxfoundation.org.)

Top 1%	$345,000 *plus*
Top 5%	$155,000
Top 10%	$112,000
Top 25%	$66,000
Top 50%	$32,000

Those numbers sure drop fast.
Guess which groups actually set goals?

3. Not many people actually set goals: <u>87%</u> have no goals at all.

    The stat doesn't say they don't have good intentions, or that they aren't working hard, it just says they don't set goals.

    Too many people are just hoping things will get better, hoping the rainbow actually has a pot of gold at the end, and are really hoping those lottery tickets pay off big time in the next drawing.

    Here we are again with that 'hope' thing. But you know what, it isn't anybody's fault, because we were not taught to prepare for real life. I don't know about you – I had to take a lot of courses in school that never really mattered, but I never got any courses on real life topics – how to prepare for a career, how to balance a checking account, how to save money – and never, ever on how to set goals and write plans so I could become successful, provide for my family and retire financially well off.

    Most people don't even know <u>what they don't know</u> about how to become successful or to plan for retirement.

4. <u>10%</u> of the people kind of have goals, but don't follow the rules.

    OK, now we're getting into the groups that really are trying to do better. They've given some thought to what they want to be, what they want to do, earn, and what direction they want to head in life – and they're putting the pedal to the metal.

    Unfortunately, this group didn't follow all the signs. Like going on a trip, they took a few wrong turns along the way because they didn't understand that not only do they need to head east to get to New York if they're in California – they need a current map, and they'll have to plan around any detours along the way.

    Goal setting is a lot like *selling.* You can be positive, work hard in sales and do OK, even without any prior planning. Goals are the same – if you take that trip in life and you work hard and give it your best shot, you will do OK in life. But without clear goals in sales and in life, OK is all you normally get.

5.   <u>Only 3%</u> of the people set goals the right way.

Now we're getting somewhere. This group takes success way past the hope system, past just working hard and having good intentions, and past those who know where they want to go, but don't know or don't follow all the rules.

This group does it right. They understand the process and the steps they have to take, and they know they'll join the 10% in the blink of an eye, unless they follow all the rules.

This book is about how to become a 3%'er!

6.   One other thing is clear in the income table: The 3% who set goals right, earn *more than <u>10</u> times* as much money as non-goal setters.

Yes, and even though that's correct and has been for as long as I've been holding classes, too many people say or think, "I don't buy it, that's just not true," and then they explain to anyone who'll listen why it isn't their fault that they aren't doing better.

7.   The 3% with goals have more $$$ than the other <u>97%</u> combined.

With stats like these, why argue? Arguing over these facts is like going to Vegas and seeing one table that almost guarantees a win and the win is 10 times bigger than every other game in the house. But instead of playing *the sure thing,* you can hear some people saying, "I don't believe it, I know what I'm doing," as they play a *hunch* and lose their money on another sucker bet.

The sucker bet in life is just working long hard days with no plan to do better. It's one thing to make poor bets in Vegas or poor decisions in life, when there's no proof of a better way.

But when the lights flash and the sirens go off on the games you choose not to play, and when there's proof like this of the benefits of setting goals for you and your family that you *choose* to ignore – you're just making very poor choices.

When you *don't know* you can do more, that's one thing and it isn't your fault. But knowing you can do better and not doing it, *is just a bad decision that will affect everyone you care about.*

8. Your activity planning is _85%_ of your success in setting clear goals, and in reaching those goals.

    Whether it's planning that trip to Hawaii, planning your income this year, or being able to retire comfortably – success hinges on all of the details in the planning stages.

    Not planning a vacation properly will just cost you a few bucks, a few headaches and a wasted week off. Not planning your year in sales will cost you that other car you need, the money to get the kids' new soccer gear and you'll have to skimp on presents at Christmas time again this year.

    A bad vacation is one of those, "Whatever!" events in life that probably won't have any long-term downside.

    Life is way more serious than a just having a bad vacation though. Not seriously planning to control your life could mean disappointment or even total disaster for you and your family.

    Life success almost always depends on your *professional success.* That's what's so great about selling. More than in almost any other profession, you can plan, prepare and execute a successful strategy in sales (and income) that leaves nothing to *hope* or *luck*.

9. When realistic goals are written with a clear plan of action and reviewed regularly, _94%_ of those goals are achieved.

    Here again, people actually argue about this, "I don't need to write my goals down, I know what I want to accomplish." This is when you want to say, "Buddy, you're having a bad dream, shake yourself and wake up before you fail."

    If you only had one goal, maybe. Even then, you'd still have to memorize the goal exactly, and memorize the plan exactly, and then you'd still need to tape reminders around the house to remind you of your goal and your plan every day.

    But with the multitude of goals you need in business and in life, there's no way you will pull that off, so what's the point in arguing? Just write your goals down and bump your odds to 94%.

10. Goal setting is a __choice__.　　　❏ I will　❏ I won't

The results are indisputable – the people who choose to set clear goals, create plans and follow their plans – achieve higher levels of success and earn more money than those who choose not to.

Goal setting works when you do it right. Because it does, that means you can choose to set goals the right way and be rewarded, or you can choose to go through life without them.

Most people in the world will never realize they have this choice in life. You do though – so choose 'goal setting' and accomplish virtually everything you want in sales, income, and in life.

If you're unsure of the real potential in this business and if you're not sure it's worth all of this trouble, order my book, "Earn Over $100,000 Every Year Selling Cars" (the information on how to order is in the back of this book) – or take the course on JVTN®.

Seriously, slow down. Speed kills sales, and speed reading kills how much you'll remember. Go back through everything we've talked about to this point, especially this chapter of facts about goal setting.

1. Grab a pen, paper and a highlighter. If you haven't already been using those learning tools so far to take notes and mark key points you want to remember – get them now.

2. Go back and circle the income group in #2 *that you're in now.*

3. Circle the income group in #2 *you want to be in.*

4. Go through each of these stats and highlight the things you know have held you back. On the paper you have, start making your 'to do' lists on becoming a goal setter. Don't worry about being neat or about being organized at this point, just make sure you note the key points, and write those down.

*Congratulations – you're already
doing something 97% of the people never do.*

"Goal setting is the closest thing there is to true magic.
Just decide what you want, write it down, create a plan to get it
and then just go to work every day and follow your plan."

– Joe Verde

Dealers & Managers

Goal setting is a 'game changer' in business and in life.

Take everything we talk about in here for salespeople and apply it to

your sales team and to the other departments in your dealership.

CHAPTER 3

THE COMMON MISTAKES
PEOPLE MAKE SETTING GOALS

The impact of goal setting is clear – if you set realistic goals, if you create a clear, logical plan of action and if you follow the plan, you'll reach your goals.

There are a lot of *ifs* in that sentence. When you look at the 97% who aren't goal setters, it really isn't that most of them aren't trying to do better for themselves and their families every day. And without question, people want to be able to retire successfully.

It's those mistakes people make along the way that stop them dead in their tracks. They accumulate so many mistakes, they never come close to achieving the things they're capable of in life or in their profession.

So let's look at those common mistakes and create *your plan* to avoid them, so you can move into that 3% group.

Common Mistakes People Make Setting Goals

1. **No Goals – Just Good Intentions, Hard Work & A Great Attitude**

Too many people confuse having good intentions, working hard, and having a great attitude about selling with having clear goals in sales. Wanting to do better is one thing and it's obviously very important. However, setting clear realistic goals and writing out and following a specific plan of action is what it takes to actually improve and grow in sales and income.

Without the specific goals and clear plans to follow, your hard work usually just wears you and your attitude down a little more each day. That's why we have so much turnover in the highest paying profession, and in the best industry you could ever want to be in – selling an *in demand* product like a car.

Everybody has a car and everybody will be getting another one, and that means you can quickly build your business if you follow the rules we'll talk about and lay out a clear plan to follow.

Life is the same – you can plan for a happy, rewarding and successful life, or be like most people who just go to work and try hard. Just like selling cars, after trying and trying and trying, one day most people just lose hope. Goals solve those problems by giving you not only a direction to follow, but by providing a checklist of the steps you need to take to get to your next level.

2. **No Starting Point**

You can't set a goal for improvement if you don't know exactly where you are now in sales or income. The only way to find your *base information* is to track (count) and average every selling opportunity, every selling activity, and your final results.

Like taking that trip to Hawaii we talked about earlier, if you're lost and don't know where you're starting from right now, good luck booking a flight to get you there.

Same thing in sales, if you don't know exactly what you're doing now, you can't set clear goals or create clear plans to do better.

3. **Goals Aren't Clear**

A lot of people (like those 10%'ers) do try to set goals, but they're too vague with their goals. They set goals like...

- I'm going to have a great month and sell a ton of cars!
- I'm going to increase my commission by $100 per unit!
- I'm going to be very successful in sales!
- I'm going to retire financially sound!

Every one of those goals is too vague. There isn't any target you can actually aim for in any of those goals. That puts you back to mistake #1, 'No goals, just good intentions.'

Instead, goals have to be very clear...

"I will deliver 22 units and I will earn at least $8,800 in commissions and bonuses by the 31st this month."

4. **Most People Include An "Out" For Missing Their Goal**

If you set a goal, and give yourself an 'out' up front, you're off the hook when you miss it and you don't even have to feel bad. You already have a pre-arranged excuse to fall back on.

Most people who do try to set goals will, out of habit, include an automatic "opt out" for not reaching their goal.

"I will deliver 22 units by the 31st <u>unless something unexpected happens.</u>"

Wow, let's see – something *unexpected* – hmmm – what could fall into the *unexpected* category?

I guess that could be anything... rain, snow, heat, cold, County Fair, kids got sick, bad back, mother-in-law moving in with you, late on bills, deals unwinding, couldn't locate a vehicle, too many customers couldn't buy, too much pressure, your daughter's soccer team won and you had to go to the big game, or just about anything else you could possibly imagine.

When you write out your goals, they have to be the 'I will do it' type, and not the 'I'll try it' kind.

5. No Written Action Plan

This is practically a default mistake from not having a clear goal. If your goal isn't clear and specific, it's next to impossible to write a plan to get you there.

Your *activities* based "Action Plan" is like a road map with the exact directions to get you to your destination.

If you're driving from Chicago to Fenway Park in Boston for a game two days from now, just saying, "I'm heading east," probably won't get you there, at least not in time for the game.

Like a map you'd need for that trip, you also need to know exactly what step to take next to keep moving toward your goals.

It's just a simple process; set a goal, take out the word 'try' and eliminate any other options for failure – then write a plan.

6. A Vague Plan

Like a vague goal, a vague plan will cost you your goal before you even start.

A plan that's too vague would be: "I will work real hard every day this month so I can reach my goal of 22 units."

Instead, be specific in your *Activity Action Plan*. Spell out exactly what you'll do to hit your 22-unit goal. How many calls will you make, how many appointments from incoming calls, prospecting, or internet leads will you make, and how many appointment 'shows' will you guarantee yourself, how many demos, and how many write ups will you do this month to hit your goal? Be specific.

And here's another 'Oops' that will trip you up – you can't write a clear plan if you don't have your exact starting point. So we're back to tracking things, in mistake #2.

Most people think tracking is too much trouble, takes too much time and doesn't matter that much anyway. At least that's what I thought my first 5 years. Then like every professional in sports, I realized I had to know exactly what I was doing today, before I could improve my performance tomorrow.

7. Setting Goals To Impress Other People

How many of those worthless highball monthly goal setting meetings have you participated in? You can hear salespeople who don't know exactly how many units they really average now, start bragging about what they'll do this month.

Manager: "Bob, you sold 8 last month, what can we count on you for this month?" "I'll do 12." "Jim, you sold 9 last month, how about you?" "If Bob can do 12, I can do 15," and the highball just keeps going around the room. By the end of the meeting, the group goal is two times what the dealership sells. So the manager says, "OK, we're going to count on you guys this month – now get out there and make me proud!"

Then on the 15th, when Bob is only at 4 (his normal half month sales) he pulls up lame on his goal, "Boss, I hit a dry spell and can't catch a decent up, plus my mother-in-law moved in with us last week, and I got that letter from the IRS again about my back taxes and that's really distracting me, too, blah, blah, blah."

So many people feel like their goal has to outdo the other guy, they never set goals they can realistically achieve. Here's a thought: Stop trying to compete with other people, and instead focus your goals on continually improving your skills, results and activities. Don't worry, *if you just keep improving,* you'll quickly pass the other salespeople.

8. "Hope" Is Not A Strategy & "Enthusiasm" Is Not A Plan

Motivation is critical to setting goals, to having the discipline to follow the plan, and it's critical to reaching your goals.

But people confuse 'Being Pumped' and hoping enthusiasm alone will carry them through to reach their goals with 'Being Prepared'. Being 'pumped' lasts hours, maybe days, but it will be your skills and habits that take you to your next level.

Go through the goal setting exercises coming up, and focus on your goals every day. If you will, you'll be motivated and excited about improving, and the best part – it won't wear off.

9. Setting Goals To Fail

When salespeople always set goals that are too high to reach, they're actually teaching themselves to fail. Why? Because the first thing you learn how to do after consistent failure is to justify why not hitting your goals is not your fault:

• We didn't have enough traffic last month to reach my goal.

• I tried, but everybody I wrote up had bad credit.

• It's a rough month and people just aren't out buying.

Set realistic goals you know you can achieve if you have a good plan. Then make a firm commitment, go to work-to-work, follow your plan and do what it takes to reach your goal.

Get my free audio download at joeverde.com/GTWTW

"Go To Work-To-Work"

10. They Refuse To Trade

Sure, most people want more, but they...

• refuse to trade in bad habits for good habits.

• won't trade the time it takes to learn and develop better skills and habits to replace their weaker skills and habits.

• won't spend the time to make the changes they have to make.

Think of your goals as *what* you want. Your action plan is your *road map* to get you there. Discipline is your *driving force*.

Selling more, earning more, doing more and retiring successfully are all easy to accomplish. Having said that, I can also tell you that *all* of your key goals will require *all* of these (and more)...

Better Skills – Better Habits – Tracking
Success Attitude – Determination – Discipline

Stop!
Review these mistakes and circle the ones you're making.
Be bold – you can't fix a mistake you won't admit to making.
If it helps to know, I've made every mistake listed, too.

CHAPTER 4

THE KEY WORDS
IN GOAL SETTING

I'm guessing you're starting to realize that there are a lot of things to learn about and to remember when it comes to setting clear goals you can actually achieve.

In this chapter, let's go over the key words you have to apply to every single goal you set.

By doing so, we can also see what really separates the high achievers in life and in sales from the rest of the people, who just wish they were more successful.

Key Words In Goal Setting

1. <u>**Realistic – Achievable – Specific – Written**</u>

   Do some people literally double or triple their sales or income overnight? Absolutely, we see it happen all the time, to people in our workshops and who are on JVTN®.

   At what selling level is that most likely to happen?

   Salespeople in the under 10-unit range can easily double or triple their sales and income right after our class. That's where they learn and develop dozens of new skills, and then go back to work-to-work with clear goals and a renewed enthusiasm for selling, and turning pro in sales.

   Common sense says it's tougher and would take longer for a 30-unit person to do the same thing because of their starting point. Can the 30-unit person still improve? Of course.

   How much can they improve? That depends on a lot of different things, but 20%, 30% or 50% are all very doable short-term goals, and the sky is the limit for them too, with effective long-term planning. (One of the last chapters explains exactly what to do.)

   You can do anything you want to do, if you plan it properly!

   Having said that, *there is no upside to setting goals that are impossible to achieve,* or goals that rely more on luck, hope, stardust or a double rainbow than probability.

   But there is a very definite downside to continually high-balling yourself on your goals. Why? Because when you regularly set unrealistic goals and miss them, you quickly develop the habit of *failing* to reach your goals instead of succeeding.

   Worse ... It won't be long before you'll just whip out your long list of reasons why missing your goals is never your fault.

   Just do it right and reach all of your goals.

   It's far better to set smaller *improvement* goals you know you can hit time after time, than to shoot for the stars and just hope something happens. If you just make sure you're always growing *some,* you'll increase your sales and income every year.

2.   Commitment

I worked with a guy who sold 8 cars every month and made a couple thousand a month. His wife got really sick and had to have emergency treatment that cost $12,000.

So how much money did he make the next month? Correct, he made a commitment, went to work and worked hard and smart to get the money he needed for her treatment. He proved he always had the ability to do more, but as soon as the urgent need went away, so did his commitment and desire to improve.

Almost everybody wants to sell more, be more, earn more and do more. The problem is *almost nobody* has the *burning desire* or the commitment it takes to pull that off consistently.

Most people can work hard and most people can also work smart. We see that every day in our business. Because they work hard or smart for awhile, almost all salespeople do have great months, and some even have great years.

But very few people work smart and hard *at the same time*. And of those who *can* work smart and hard, 97% just can't seem to work smart and hard at the same time *long enough* to develop the skills and work habits to continually improve.

More Success Requires A Sustained Commitment.
You *can* sell more and earn more, and when you actually
make the commitment to improve every year – you will!

3.   Discipline

Creating a goal and developing a plan of action are the easy parts of goal setting, but *reaching goals* requires the heavy lifting most people just aren't willing to do. Let's look at the process of setting a goal, writing a plan and then following the plan.

A. My Goal...

"I will improve my sales by 50% this quarter by assuming everyone can and will buy, by giving 80% a great demonstration of the product, and by mastering the Landmark Close, Sold Line Close, my Action Closes and the Final Wrap Up."

B. My Activity Action Plan for ___ / ___ (this month / year)...

❑ Track every opportunity I have on the lot, so I can accurately measure my 80% demo goal.

❑ Write out 20 Open-Ended questions to build rapport.

❑ Write out 20 Either / Or questions to investigate to find my customer's wants and needs.

❑ Write out 20 "Yes" questions to confirm the benefits of the features during my presentation.

❑ Review and practice all of the recommendations in the "How To Sell More Cars" course on JVTN® on how to get everyone on a demonstration drive.

❑ With a partner, practice my presentation to the Secondary Driver when I first trade drivers.

❑ With a partner, practice my presentation to the Primary Driver when it's their turn to drive.

❑ Write out 20 Summary "Yes" questions I can use in the Landmark Close.

❑ Write out my Assumptive Sold Line Close.

❑ Write out 6 Action Closes I can use with every customer, and 6 more for when the customer has a trade-in.

❑ Write out my Wrap Up – the Silent Walk Around, the questions I'll ask about the mileage they drive, their MPG and any maintenance they've done to their vehicle.

❑ Write out 6 different Final Closing questions – two each on Registration, Refreshment and Accessories.

❑ With a partner, practice everything above out loud focusing on my tone, inflection and delivery at least 3 times each day for 30 days – first thing in the morning, again during the day, and before I leave the dealership.

So is it worth it to do all of that in '3B' to reach your goal?

Would a 50% improvement in units and income in the next 90 days be worth your time to set clear goals and then do everything in your Activity Plan to reach your goals?

In real life, not to most people. They blow it off as impossible or laugh it off as something they really don't care about, even when the fridge is empty and little Johnny needs new shoes.

Can you believe it ... some salespeople will even talk about how impossible something is, while they're standing next to someone else who is doing exactly what they're explaining can't be done.

It's a given that a 10-car guy can get to 20. The real challenge in hitting a 50% improvement is ... are they willing to develop the same skills and work habits of the 20-car guy, and do they have the discipline to work hard and smart at the same time, long enough to make it happen every day?

Congratulations again! I know you're interested in doing better or you wouldn't still be reading this book. So stop and think about where you'd normally drop the ball in your planning and make getting past that hurdle your next goal.

4.   Enthusiasm

Your enthusiasm may be last on this list, but it's as important or maybe even more important than everything else.

Why? Because enthusiasm is 80% of the sale – whether you're talking about selling a vehicle to your next customer or selling yourself on becoming more successful.

If you make goal setting something that you like to do, want to do and enjoy doing because of the benefits for you and your family – you'll consistently set and reach your goals. And once you make goal setting a regular part of your life personally and professionally, it will change your life for the better.

I know this makes sense, but what about those days when you just aren't excited about following the plan? That's easy...

Just act enthusiastic and you'll be enthusiastic. – Dale Carnegie

Improvement vs. A Good Month

I've read this next comment stated many different ways in sports about *winning versus being a champion...*

"In sports, you can get lucky and win a game or even a title, but in most sports, you aren't considered a real champion until you have defended your title successfully."

Isn't that also true in sales? You can be the worst salesperson in town and still have a great or even a record month. But if you fall back to where you were, it was just that, a record month and nothing to write home about after that one event.

Just like in sports, long-term success in sales means being able to consistently produce at a professional level month after month, not just having a good month now and then.

When you have a good month, that's great – and I'm sure not suggesting that getting lucky isn't good, we all appreciate it. But 'growing' is a continuous *process.*

A good month is an event – it's not growth.

Growth is when you have a good month and then a better month and continually *more* better months.

You can learn how to double or triple your sales or income through goal setting. I know you can, because I personally increased my sales to 5 times higher than before, and we see it happen all the time, when people get serious after our classes or with JVTN®. Double or triple or higher is always possible.

One of the challenges in learning to set goals and in growing, is keeping all this from sounding so difficult you don't do it. Hang in there and don't let that happen, because getting everything you want in life is a simple 3-step process...

Set a goal – make a plan – work your plan.

CHAPTER 5

TWO TYPES OF GOALS
YOU HAVE TO SET

Think about it. One type of goal you'll set is on what you want to happen, that's a *result goal*.

A result goal ... "I will deliver 22 units this month and I will earn $13,500 in commissions and bonuses."

Then you'll need to set *activity goals,* so that you can achieve those results ...

An activity goal ... "I'll avoid talking price and focus on value, I'll give 80% of my prospects a demonstration, and I'll write up 75% of those people."

You will always have your *'what I want to happen'* results goals in many different areas.

And you will always need your *'how I'm going to make it happen'* activity goals to reach each result goal.

The key to success in sales is to learn to manage your *activities* because your *results* will always follow.

Result vs. Activity Goals

"Verde, get out there and go sell something."

My manager used to say that all the time when he'd see me with a cup of coffee or just standing around. The problem is you don't just 'go sell a car'. You have to remember that selling a car is the end result, it's not what you need to do first to make it happen.

A slightly better direction he could have given me would have been, "Go *do something* to sell a car." OK, there's a little more clarity to 'do something to sell' instead of just 'go sell a car'. That still won't work though, because it doesn't clearly define exactly what you would need to do so you end up with a delivery.

A more specific direction would be to focus on the specific *activities* you need to do that will result in a sale...

"Go find somebody on the lot, follow all of the steps to selling, get a commitment, write them up so we have a chance to sell a car. If there's nobody on the lot right now, either pick up the phone and contact everyone you didn't sell this month and try to set a firm appointment, or contact a repeat customer and ask for a referral and focus on setting a firm appointment, or walk out to the Service Drive, engage a customer in conversation and use the Service Satisfaction Referral Script so you can generate a lead for a sale in the future, or bring them up front for a presentation on the spot."

You manage your sales by managing your activities.

So remember – to sell more, earn more and grow every year, you have to learn how to set two types of goals...

    A. Result Goals ... the end result – what you want to happen.

    B. Activity Goals ... what you'll do to make it happen.

That means the real *secret* to success in sales is learning how to manage your *activities* every day, so you are either selling a car right now, or generating a lead or an appointment for tomorrow.

Three different ways you can increase your sales...

Here's an example of why knowing exactly what you do each month is so critical to improving.

Let's say you've been accurately tracking your opportunities, your activities and your results. You've found that over the last three months, each month you've been averaging...

• 60 Opportunities	People you talked to on the lot
• 40 Demos	You gave 66% a demonstration
• 20 Write Ups	You wrote up 50% of your demos You wrote up 33% of opportunities
• 10 Deliveries	You closed 50% of write ups, 25% of demos and 20% of all opportunities.

Now you know your *current 3-month average* in those 4 categories and you know your closing ratio. Improving your results – your deliveries and income – is now just a simple *math problem.*

Option #1: Demo more and you'll sell more!

With the information (above) on your average number of demos and deliveries, fill in the blank below on the change you could make in *just* your number of demonstrations, so you would deliver 12 units instead of 10, *without talking to more people.*

Right now you deliver 25% of your demos. So how many demos would you have to give to deliver 12 units instead of 10? _____

If you said 48 demos, you're right.

You could deliver 2 more units and increase your income accordingly, just by learning how to get 80% of the people you already talk to behind the wheel instead of just 66%. Your numbers would change to 60 opportunities – 48 demos – 24 write ups – 12 deliveries.

Option #1 is *just one way* to increase your sales and income without working longer or having to talk to more people – *there's more...*

Option #2: Write up more prospects and you'll sell more!

Fill in the blank below on the change you could make in *just* your number of write ups so you would deliver 12 units, *without talking to more people.*

Now ... You deliver 50% of your write ups. So how many write ups would you need to deliver 12 units instead of just 10? _____

If you said 24, you'd be correct. You could deliver 2 more units each month just by not prequalifying, by developing a more effective closing process to end up writing 60% of your demos.

So by tracking what you do, you know *exactly which activities* to adjust to increase your sales and income without talking to more people.

Option #3: What if you demonstrated 80% and wrote up 60%?

If you did 80% demos and 60% write ups, how many would you sell then? Correct: 14.5, and you'd sell those extra 4.5 units without coming in early or staying late. You're able to increase your units and income by knowing exactly which activities to improve.

Believe it – selling more and earning more is just a math problem.

- Track everything you do, set your Results Goals, and then adjust your Activities to drive you to those results.

- Learn to use these two types of goals together, and you'll be able to almost completely control your career in sales.

"From 8 to 38.5"

"When I first started selling cars my average was 8 per month. In the last two years I have attended 2 Joe Verde Workshops, I use his Monthly Planning Guides daily and I use his VSA® (Mini-CRM in JVTN®) to manage my customers.

Now my 90-day average is 38.5!

I do well because I eat, live and breathe Joe Verde methods, training and processes. I am proof it works and I can honestly say I do not know where I would be without Joe!"

– Trent, Salesperson, Chevrolet, Utah

CHAPTER 6

How Far Into The Future Should You Set Goals?

The answer requires a second question...

How far do you want to get in life?

If you can buy into the fact that your goals drive your success, then by default you accept the fact that when you stop setting goals to grow and improve, you stop growing and improving in the future.

NASA has goals hundreds of years into the future. If you think about it, even a rocket scientist can't just wake up one day and say, "Hey – I have an idea, let's shoot a rocket to Mars today, who wants to light it?"

You may not be able to pinpoint 30-year goals, but it makes sense to do a rough sketch of how you'd like to see your future play out, so you can start to control it.

Goal Setting Time Frames

1. **How far into the future should you think about setting goals, and where should you start?**

    Grab a telescope and let's get started.

    A. Start with your ___Lifetime Goals___ .

    Now ————————————————→ **Lifetime**

    Everything should start with your *vision* of what you want to accomplish in life. But most of us don't really know exactly what we want the rest of our lives to look like.

    A vision is just that – it's vague, you know the general direction, just not the exact spot. Like deciding to go to the movies – you're not sure what you want to see, so you figure it out when you get to the theatre and see what's playing. Or let's say you decide, "I will own my own dealership 20 years from now." While not totally specific, it is *generally* specific and having that general goal will definitely help you get moving in the right direction. The clarity and the specifics will come later, once you set these first goals.

    B. Then back your Lifetime goals into Long-Term Goals .

    Now ———→ **Long-Term** ———→ Lifetime

    Long-term goals are steps to your lifetime goals and these start a year from now (from today's date) and they can be 1, 2, 5 and maybe 10-year goals, but not much further out.

    Lifetime goals are vague, but long-term goals are close enough to become those clear goals you can almost touch, and they're critical to consistent growth, year after year. These are your stepping stones to lifetime goals.

    You'll see this as we go along, but if you really learn how to set goals correctly, you'll never arrive at your final destination. *Why?* Because you don't set just one 5-year goal, you keep re-setting new 5-year goals to keep you moving forward.

C. Next come your <u>Intermediate or Medium-Term Goals</u>.

Now   ⟶   **Medium**   ⟶   Long   ⟶   Lifetime

Intermediate goals take you from 90 days up to one year. They're the stepping stones to reach your long-term goals. If you're at 10 units now and you want to average 22 one year from now, you just break your goal into segments.

10 Now   ⟶   13 @ 3 Mo.   ⟶   16 @ 6 Mo.   ⟶   22 @ 1 Yr.

To be at 22 in a year, you'll need to average 16 in 6 months (medium) and 13 units 3 months from now (short).Then you'll break those goals down to monthly and daily activities you focus on in your Activity Action Plan each day.

D. Last are your <u>Short-Term Goals</u>.

Now ⟶ **Short** ⟶ Medium ⟶ Long ⟶ Lifetime

Short-term goals start from right now and focus through the next 90 days. These are your immediate, first steps.

Using the 22 goal breakdown above, you'll need to *average just one more unit each month*. Sure seems realistic to me.

E. <u>Annual Goals</u> (A completely different category).

January ⟶ December

These are annual improvement goals. You need them so you can increase your sales and income every year *on purpose*.

Oops! One of the biggest mistakes dealers, managers and salespeople make in goal setting is they *only set annual goals*.

Why is it a problem? Because you need overlapping goals to keep moving forward. With *only* annual goals, on December 31st, you're done. You haven't thought about next year's goals, so you wake up January 1st with no goals.

2. **How often should you review and reset your goals?**

   A. Lifetime goal setting isn't just a once in a lifetime event. You need to review lifetime goals at least every 5 years.

   Why? Because things change, especially when you become a goal setter and start improving. I can promise the visions of the future you see today will change dramatically, as you start reaching your goals. As you grow and improve, so will your long-range vision and planning.

   Let's say you sell 10 units now and are making $30,000 a year. Letting your mind wander, you figure you'd like to make $100,000 a year by the time you retire and that you'd like to have your house and car paid off and have $50,000 in the bank. Today, that seems like a grand plan for retirement.

   I can guarantee you that as you start setting goals correctly, writing effective activity plans, getting the sales education you'll need, and following your plans, it will feel like you just got out of an economy car and into a race car.

   If you take goal setting seriously, within a year you'll most likely be earning more than $8,333 per month. That means you'll already be on track by the end of this year to make $100,000 or more the following year.

   Whether you end up hitting $50,000, $75,000 or $100,000+ the first year you start setting goals, all of your future sales goals, including your lifetime goals, will need a bump.

   So how often should you reset your lifetime goals?

   In general, you'll want to take a hard look at your lifetime goals every 5 years. Sooner if you're going gangbusters on improvements and growth. Look at where you are at that point, also look at what's going on in your life besides selling (kids, more kids, grandkids, new house, etc.) and then adjust your lifetime goals from there.

☞ Tip: Put a recurring event in your phone calendar every 5 years to remind yourself to review and adjust your lifetime goals.

B1. Long-Term, 2-5-10-year goals should be reviewed annually.

Short	Medium / Intermediate	Long
Now – 3 Mo.	3 Months – 1 Year	1 Year – 5 Year – 10 Year

Long-term goals are the break points in your lifetime plans. These goals take you from over a year up to a 10-year goal.

A 5 or 10-year goal may not be crystal clear, but those goals definitely start to clarify that general lifetime plan you originally started with. Before long, you'll be able to see your lifetime goals just as clearly as your 5-year goals, and that's when you really get excited.

B2. Long-Term, 1-Year Goals should be reviewed quarterly.

Why B1 & B2? Because the long-term range is so broad. Remember, long-term is anything from a year all the way to those lifetime goals. That means when you're talking about a 1-year goal, it will be much more specific than a 10-year goal.

It may be hard to believe, but if you set realistic long-term goals, work them backwards into medium and short-term goals, create a daily plan and follow it – you'll be blowing past your goals left and right, especially your first few years.

In fact, here's a realistic example...

If you're selling 10 units now, and you buckle down, set goals and start training 30 minutes a day, you'll be shocked at just how easy you'll double your sales overnight.

You can easily go from 10 units to 20 in 90 days or less in *several different ways,* so just check one and get to work...

❑ Work. The average salesperson puts in a 9-hour shift each day, but only *works* 3 of those 9 hours (doing something to sell a car right now, or something to generate a sale in the future). Just go to work-to-work and double sales.

It's just math – if you work 3 hours and sell 10, just *work* 6 hours instead and sell 20. That's how the 30-car guys sell 30. They've learned to *work* all 9 hours of their 9-hour day.

❑ Do more demonstrations and better presentations. Right now the average salesperson only gives 4 out of 10 people who show any interest in a vehicle, a demonstration. We know 99% won't buy without a demo, and we also know that 50% of the people who *do* get a great presentation and demonstration, buy on the spot.

Stop trying to guess 'who' can or will buy before you give them the *value reasons* to buy. Just assume every customer can and will buy, and give 8 out of 10 instead of just 4 out of 10 a great demonstration, and you will double your sales, without spending any more time at work.

❑ Follow up with everyone who doesn't buy.

78% of the people who look at a vehicle do buy, and 90% buy within a week of stopping at the first dealership.

Easy math – 8 out of 10 do buy, 7 buy within a week. If you close 20% (2 out of 10), that means you miss 6 out of every 8 sales you could have had.

Problem / Opportunity – 90% who don't buy are never contacted again. If you aren't following up your unsold prospects, if you'll just get contact information on 75% of them before they leave, and make 3 contacts to each the way we teach, you'll increase your sales 67% immediately.

This change alone will take you from 10 units now to 17 units, without spending more time at work.

❑ Learn to prospect by phone and out in Service.

How long does a 5-minute prospecting call take?

Correct – about 5 minutes. To get from 10 to 20, just make 10 of those 5-minute calls every day and follow the steps and the words *exactly* that are in our Referral Script.

Also, go to Service each day and meet just 2 people and use our Service Survey Script *exactly* the way we teach it.

Now it just a math problem again. You're talking to 12 more people per day than you normally would. That's 60 more people per week, and 240 more per month. Statistically, 30% of them have a family member who will trade within the next 90 days. That's 72 *extra buyers* you'll bump into, every single month, and that means more sales.

❑ Learn to close the sale. You can also just learn how to avoid price, sell value, and learn to close the sale, overcome objections and set up an easy *budget-focused* negotiation, instead of heading into a price-dropping marathon.

Just spend 30 days on developing your selling skills in the process we teach. That course on JVTN® is titled, "How To Sell More Cars". Develop those skills, learn the closes in that course, give everyone your best shot and you'll be staring at 20 to 30 units on your paycheck instead of 10, and shaking your head, because it was always that easy.

❑ Or here's a thought – instead of picking just one of the above to get from 10 to 20, just do *everything above,* and head straight to 30 or 40 units like so many other people do after our classes and courses on JVTN® (which I'm guessing most of you have in your dealership now).

OK, let's say you set an extremely realistic goal to get from 10 now, to 20 in one year. Great news – if you do everything we just talked about, you'll most likely be at 20 units 3 months from now. That's great, but it also voids your 1-year goal because you already reached it. Now you need a new goal, even though you just set a 1-year goal 3 months ago.

Sure, it happened fast, but now you're a 20-car guy, not a 10-car guy. What's realistic 1-year from now? Yes, you had a big first bump, and if you continue to apply yourself, is there any logical reason to believe you couldn't average selling at least 25 per month within the next 12 months?

Here again, if you train and work smart, you can expect to blow past that goal in under 12 months, too. That's why I recommend you *update your 1-year goals every quarter.*

☞ Add another event in your calendar at the beginning of each quarter: *"Review my one-year goal."*

C. Review your Intermediate goals quarterly or monthly.

Short	Medium / Intermediate	Long
Now – 3 Mo.	3 Months – 1 Year	1 year – 5 Year – 10 Year

Intermediate goals are just that – they're in between your short and long-term goals. If your goal is to get from 10 to 22 in one year, then math says you need to be at 16 within 6 months to be on track and just at 13 in three months.

These shorter goals are constantly changing, and you'll adjust your Intermediate Goals and your Action Plans to keep you on track each time you adjust your long-term goals.

"Adjust your goals" begs the question...

Should you lower your goals if you aren't on track?

NO! If you started with a realistic goal, instead of lowering it, adjust your activities to a higher level and work harder on your skills, work habits and your choice of customers.

D. Review your Short-Term goals every month.

Short	Medium / Intermediate	Long
Now – 3 Mo.	3 Months – 1 Year	1 year – 5 Year – 10 Year

These become your 90-day goals, your monthly goals, and your weekly and daily goals, and part of your activity plan.

Remember, salespeople don't have bad months or bad years. They just allow themselves to accumulate too many bad days that create those bad months and bad years.

Your clearly defined goals and your activity plans practically guarantee you'll eliminate the bad months. Why? Because you're focusing every day on the steps to reach your short, intermediate and long-term goals.

To set your short-term goals, just work your Results Goal backward – then create your Action Plan of monthly, weekly and daily *minimum activities and minimum training* that will take you straight to your goals.

☞ Adjust your short-term goals *monthly* as needed.

E. Review your Annual Goals at the end of each quarter.

JAN	FEB	**MAR**	APR	MAY	**JUN**	JUL	AUG	**SEP**	OCT	NOV	**DEC**

Of course, you want to also set an annual *improvement* goal so that you're continually and consistently improving your sales volume and your income, year after year.

Read it again – I said, "Set an annual *improvement* goal." That means you need to have a *record* year, *every year.*

I really hope you're starting to see that breaking records every year is possible. When I first started working, I was 6 or 7, doing chores on the farm and picking cotton with my grandparents. At 8, I was plowing the field (probably kinda crooked). At 12 or 13, I started working (for money) by plowing fields for my uncle after school and at night.

Ever since I started earning money, I've made more money every year except for 3 or 4, in total. In the last 27 years of business, we've had a record year 24 of those 27 years.

We all have to work every day, whether we earn a little or a lot. I'm not money-hungry – but if I have to go to work anyway, I just choose to go to work-to-work, to do my very best every single day. By doing that, I'm able to set records every year.

> *Trap ... It's easy to think you can blow off a day here and there and assume, "I will make it up tomorrow!"*

Too many people in sales take *today* casually. They really do figure all these deals they don't push extra hard for today will just come in tomorrow or that they can work extra hard next week to make up for what they didn't do this week.

> *Please note: In life or sales, there are no make-up days.*

You can't replace what you didn't do yesterday, even if you have a great day today. Yesterday is gone. It's in the history books and so are all the opportunities yesterday offered.

Treat every day as though it's the last day of the year, and you'll reach levels in sales and income you never thought were possible.

Are you in this rut...?

Did you know that by the time we're 30 years old, 80% of us have narrowed our overall attitudes, we've stopped developing new skills and we've developed so many habits we just continually repeat, that we've practically locked ourselves into a personal, financial and career rut that we'll spend the rest of our lives in.

That is – unless you become a goal setter!

CHAPTER 7

THE STEPS TO CONTROLLING YOUR CAREER WITH GOALS

We clearly explain the steps to selling in our classes and on JVTN®, that you can follow to deliver a vehicle more than 50% of the time. Those steps have to be taken in order to hit 50% though, but most salespeople are in a hurry, they leave out some of the steps and miss sales.

When a builder builds a house, the foundation is first, then the framing, roof, electrical, plumbing, wiring, walls, flooring, fixtures. etc. and final details. They don't change the order of their steps either, because that order guarantees a better built house that will last longer, built in less time, at a lower cost.

Goal setting is also a step-by-step process. If you follow these steps, you'll be doing what the top 3% do to reach their goals, and you are guaranteed to improve.

The Ten Steps To Becoming A Goal Setter...

Follow These Steps Exactly

1. **Fire up your ___imagination___ .**

   Believe it or not, this is one of the toughest, yet most critical steps in goal setting for most people. It's tough for most people to learn how to start daydreaming again.

   Why is it so tough? Psychologists tell us by the time we're 7 or 8 years old, most of us have lost most or all of our imagination. They also tell us by the time we're 30, almost all of us are locked into a mental rut and have developed so many habits, we don't change or grow past them, we just get older.

   How and why does that happen? Well, if you think about it, by 7 or 8 we've heard, "You can't do that / that won't work / don't even bother trying / you're wasting your time / that's a stupid idea / etc." so many times, we've just stopped even trying new things. By the time we're 30, we've heard 'you can't do it' repeated again and again. So why try, we can't do it anyway.

   Goal setters are dreamers though, and if you can't *mentally see yourself* doing more, achieving more, having more, earning more, etc. – it just won't happen, it can't. You have to see it and believe it, or you're unlikely to ever achieve it.

   The purpose in this first step is to help fire up your imagination again. It's a critical step in learning to set goals.

   This is your homework right now or tonight...

   a. Get a pen and paper, *not a computer for this,* and find a quiet spot – no kids, no TV, no distractions.

   b. Make a list of anything and everything you'd like to have, see, do or be. Kind of like that "bucket list" we talk about. Don't worry about whether it's realistic or not. If you wished you owned a jet or had enough petty cash to write a check to pay off the deficit, then write it down.

   c. Your minimum goal is 25 items and there is no maximum. If you want it, write it down. Try to list 100 or more.

2.   **Now it's time to ___prioritize___ the items on your list.**

This is easy, too. Now you're just going to put each item on your list into three groups: 1) the things that are really important to you, 2) the things that are kind of important to you, and 3) the things that are just fun to think about. Beside each item on your list, put a 1, 2 or 3.

- 1's are the most important. These are the things you need, want or would really like to do or be.

- 2's are sort of important. These are the things that would be nice to do or nice to have.

- 3's are total daydreams. These are just fun to think about and want, but really don't matter.

Keep this list forever. No, seriously, forever. Get a 3-ring binder and make it your goal setting and goal planning log. I promise that years from now when you look back at this sheet, it will bring a smile to your face to realize that you hit all of your 1's, or they're still in progress, you hit a lot of the 2's you'd rated *nice* to have, and you'll be shocked to see that you've actually hit some of those 3's that were just fun things to list.

3.   **The 1's are most important, so now put a ___date___ beside each of the 1's for when you'd like to hit that goal.**

OK, you've labeled them and now it's time to start putting them in order, based on when you want to accomplish each of them.

This group will include your sales and income goals, as well as the personal and other things you want to accomplish.

Just put the date you plan to hit each of the priority things on your list. Later, we'll take those 1's and start creating clear goals and start writing plans to get you there.

Tip: I don't show other people my goals, except for the goals they're actually involved in, *unless I know they'll support me 100%.*

Why? Because not everyone will be positive about your goals. You've already heard, "You can't," enough times in your life already. You only need to focus on, "I can," right now.

4. **Find your ___baseline___ on all sales related 1's.**

From your tracking (coming up soon), find your current averages in those 1's that are sales related, so you have your *baseline* as your starting point for a short, intermediate or long-term goal.

As you read through this book, I've included a lot of average baseline statistics you can use if you haven't been tracking. But *only use those as your first guidelines.* The key to your growth is to know exactly what *your results* are in sales every month.

You'll also need to find your baseline in the related *activities* so you know exactly where to improve there, too. Example: If your goal is to increase your sales from 10 to 20, you'll need to know...

• How many people you're talking to now each month, and the type of prospect (Up, Repeat, Referral, Dealership Customer, Incoming Call / Internet Lead, etc.)

• How many prospecting calls you make, emails you send and receive, and your percentage of unsold follow up contact information, and actual follow up contacts each month.

• How many incoming calls and leads you get (exactly), how many appointments you set from those calls and leads, and how many of those actually *show up* on the lot.

• Your averages in demos and write ups, deliveries, gross profit, commissions, bonuses, spiffs and factory cash.

5. **Turn your 1's into result goals and be very ___specific___ .**

Do not use ... "I want" – "I could" – "I'll try".

Use these words instead, and check off when completed...

❑ I will earn $30,000 in the first quarter of this year
❑ I will average 20 units per month by June 30th
❑ I will raise my average to 22 units by September 30th
❑ I will average 25 units per month by December 31st
❑ I will earn $140,000 this year

There's no trying in goal setting – just doing!

6. **Write out an "Activity" ___Action___ Plan for each goal.**

Using your activity averages in #4, now set activity goals that will drive you to those goals.

Here are some examples...

❑ I will complete at least one chapter of the selling process, closing process, or unsold follow up process on JVTN® daily.

❑ I will complete all of the related homework and practice what is recommended in each training chapter I complete.

❑ I will go to work-to-work every day and I will use 100% of my shift effectively to make a sale now or in the future.

❑ I will make 10 prospecting calls each day to my previous customers, orphan owners, or my friends and acquaintances.

❑ I will meet at least 2 people in Service each day and use Joe's service drive referral script exactly.

❑ I will get contact information on 75% of the people I don't sell, I will master Joe's follow up process and call them.

❑ I will master, and then complete every step in the Wander Around stage of the selling process with every prospect.

❑ I will master the demo and I will demonstrate the vehicle to 80% of the people I talk to each month.

❑ I will master and then follow the closing process in steps 5, 6, 7 & 8 of The New Basics™, 100% of the time.

❑ I will master my closing and objection handling skills and I will write up 75% of the people I demo each month.

❑ I will spend any extra time I need to and fully develop the skills above, so I can reach my goals.

7. **Make a ___total commitment___ with no options for failure.**

Write this down and read it 10 times each day:

*I will follow every step of my action plans
and I will reach every goal I set!*

8. **Give yourself a   <u>reward</u>   for reaching each goal.**

You don't have to buy a new car or go on a vacation every time you hit your goals, but do something to reward yourself and your family when you reach goals. It doesn't have to be a big reward – a dinner, a movie or a family day would be great.

9. ** <u>Review</u>   your goals every day.**

The more often you review your goals, the quicker and easier it will be to reach them.

If your *realistic goal* is to raise your current average to 20 units per month, 6 months from now, and your reward is a vacation...

• Go online and gather all of the information you'll need

• Select the date, book your tickets and print your itinerary

• Print pictures of the hotel you'll be staying at

• Get copies of the brochure for horseback riding, hiking and the helicopter ride you'll take everyone on

Then, whether your goal is that vacation, a car, or a new house, get all of the pictures and information and tape it on the refrigerator or somewhere everyone in the family can see every day.

By posting family rewards, you can bet your spouse and kids will be your cheerleaders at home, always trying to help and encourage you. The best news – when you get everyone involved in your goal and the reward, you will definitely *work* your shift.

Also, write your 20-unit goal on some 3 x 5 cards and tape one to the refrigerator, and keep one in your pocket. Every month on JVTN® you'll also be reminded to set your goal, and every time you log into JVTN®, you'll *see* an update on your progress.

10. **Keep the   <u>faith</u> .**

The last dealership I worked at was very demotivating, but it was close to home, with a great product and the pay plan was good (except for the pay cuts I got every time I sold more).

I had to take goal setting and motivating myself into my own hands. So I got a flip chart to use at home and created my own goal setting temperature bulb and filled it in, every time I sold another car and made another commission.

One month I had a $10,000 goal and I was literally $6,000 away from hitting it with just a week left in the month. But I had faith, because I was doing all of my activities, and then some.

The last week of the month it rained deals and money from all my activities, and I ended up closer to $11,000 than $10,000.

If you use your tracking as a guide, you'll know what to expect from your activities. So if you have a realistic goal, if you've written a good plan and if you're doing those activities every day, just keep the faith. Worse case, because you're managing your activities, if you don't hit your goal, hang on – because all those activities will hit next month and it will be awesome.

Trust the process – it works 94% of the time.

Will You 'Do It'...or... Will You 'Try It'?

An expedition was organized to climb the north wall of the Matterhorn; which had never been done. So reporters were interviewing climbers who were from around the world.

A reporter asked one man, "Are you going to climb the north wall?" The man replied, "I'm going to give it everything I have."

The reporter asked a second climber, "Are you going to climb the north wall of the Matterhorn?" The climber answered, "I'm going to do the very best I can."

Still another was asked if he was going to climb the north wall and he said, "I'm going to give it my very best effort."

The reporter asked another young man, "Are you going to climb the north wall?" This man looked him dead center and said, "I will climb the north wall of the Matterhorn."

Only one man succeeded that day – the one who said, "I will!"

They don't keep score in my grandson's soccer league. No team is allowed to win, and everybody gets a blue ribbon, gold star or trophy for playing – just to make sure they all feel good.

A lot of people reading this have also gotten used to getting a pat on the back, passing grades, blue ribbons and those same trophies all of their life, too.

You can accomplish anything you want, and you can be anything or anybody you want to be. But I have to warn you there won't be a trophy or a pat on the back, and you sure won't get that awesome house, that fancy car, retire financially sound, or fill up your kids' college fund just because you make an *appearance* or just *try* at work or in life.

Those kinds of rewards require real goals, real plans, real skills and self-discipline, day in and day out, the rest of your life.

Become a goal setter and make today the first day
that you take complete control of the rest of your life.

CHAPTER 8

THE SHORTCUTS TO
REACHING YOUR GOALS FASTER

I'm guessing if you've never really been a goal setter and if you're reading this all the way through in one sitting – this is either sounding like...

> • A gold mine just waiting to be worked

> • Or way too much to learn and do

I'd have to agree on both counts. I'm a goal setter and I'm writing this book – and at times I'm thinking, "Holy smokes, this sounds tough to understand."

So slow down. Goal setting really is easy. You have to get it right though, so you can join the 3% at the top instead of the 10% that almost make it.

I'll show you some shortcuts next, but I suggest you finish this book and then read it again, and again.

How To Hit Your Goals Faster

1. Realistic & Achievable

If you think about it, there are two things that really make a goal Realistic and Achievable. Those would be...

- The *time frame* you give yourself to reach the goal, and
- The *effort* you're willing to put in to hitting your goal.

Good: Most people in sales are driven by instant gratification. We meet a stranger at the curb and want to earn a commission in just a couple of hours for doing a great job.

Bad: That reason we're in sales is also one of our biggest enemies to growing and improving. *We want everything now.*

For example: If you're selling 10 now, 30 is definitely possible in 90 days, 6 months, or by the end of the year. It's just not realistic for *most* people to triple their sales by the end of the month.

Too many salespeople do the opposite and boldly announce, "I'm gonna deliver 30 this month." When it doesn't happen, they're bummed and explain why it wasn't their fault. Worse, too many throw in the towel on ever trying to improve again.

Base every goal on your 90-day current averages, not just where you think you are, then consider the *time frame* for your goal, and how much *effort* you'll put in to reaching the goal.

2. Develop Your Skills

Because you're in sales, and because selling relies on skills, every *result* goal you set, and every *activity* goal in your *activity action plan* will require several *skills* to achieve. Examples...

- Goal: Sell more of the prospects I already talk to on the lot.

  Skills ... You'll have to develop your questioning skills to build rapport, investigate and give targeted presentations, plus learn how to listen to your customer's wants and needs to build value, and you'll also need to improve your selling, closing, and objection handling skills to get a commitment.

- Goal: Raise the gross to improve your commission.

  Skills ... You need all of the skills to sell more, plus skills to *bypass* price on the lot, *rephrase* price when you're closing, and *refocus* price in the negotiation, plus negotiation skills.

- Goal: Sell more of your unsold prospects (get more be-backs).

  Skills ... Same thing – you need questioning skills to get the contact info, learn how to handle price on the phone, plus your closing and objection skills to close on an appointment.

- Goal: Build your repeat business.

  Skills ... You'll need to develop your organizational skills, your first 45-day sold customer follow up skills and process, plus develop your ongoing retention process.

- Goal: Prospect by phone and in Service.

  Skills ... You need to master the referral script, your questioning skills to investigate, build rapport, close on an appointment, better organizational skills and a process you follow each time.

- Goal: Sell more incoming phone and internet leads.

  Skills ... Develop your questioning skills to investigate and control the call, avoid price, handle color and equipment questions, learn to *expand* your inventory, close on a firm appointment, anchor the appointment and develop your organizational skills and incoming call and lead process.

I hope you're starting to see what I mean when I say that your *skills* will always come into play on just about any type of sales volume or income goal you set. (Take the courses on JVTN®.)

Those are just your *core* skills. Then you have other JVTN® courses on selling used cars, working special weekend events and big sales, and dozens of specific methods to handle buying objections, close sales, set up negotiations, handle trade expectations, control the negotiation, plus down, payment and all of the other price-type of objections that come up.

You need all of these skills in sales and to get them, and keep them, you need daily practice so you're always ready to sell.

3. Speed Kills Skill Development

I was talking to a dealer yesterday who was excited because one of his salespeople had already watched 100 chapters, in just the first 30 days they had JVTN® at their dealership.

To most people that would sound awesome, and I agree – he has a very motivated salesperson. The problem is – the goal isn't to power watch videos. Why? Because just watching videos doesn't help you develop the skills you need to grow and improve.

The goal with training, in our classes or on JVTN® isn't to just *watch* the class or video. It's to *take the courses,* so you can *develop your skills*. You won't develop any goal setting skills by just reading this book, either. You'll gain new information, and you'll learn how to set goals – but developing and improving your actual skills? No, those take practice and application.

If you really break down one of our 10-minute chapters online, most chapters usually have 2 or 3 days of practice time needed to complete the chapter and develop even *first-level skills*.

For example: I can write out the entire 5-question referral script in less than half a page. You can read it, but to really master just those five questions with the correct words, correct tone and inflection and the correct overall body language, will take you at least a week of practice, if you work hard on it every day.

> *To most people that sounds like too much work,*
> *but think about what it could mean to your sales...*

In less than one week, you can master one of the most critical skills that will control the rest of your career in sales. And if every type of question, every method to overcome an objection, every script to control a phone call or schedule an appointment that actually shows up takes you a full week – in just one year, you'll have developed 52 critical skills as a salesperson.

That's why in class and in my books, "Earn Over $100,000 Selling Cars" and, "How To Sell Cars", we remind everyone...

> *If you'll work harder than anybody else will for just*
> *one year to develop your skills – you'll earn more than*
> *anybody else can the rest of your career. – Joe*

By the way, you also have to maintain your skills.

I'm sure you've all heard the old story about how you need to keep your axe sharp if you're a wood cutter. Well, the same is true in sales. At the same time you're developing new skills, you're also losing the edge on almost every skill you already had.

Earlier I said we've grown 24 of 27 years at JVG, and that our average salesperson has been with us over 10 years, some more than 15. What I didn't say is we train all of our very experienced high achievers in sales every day for 45 minutes *before* we start work. Every salesperson goes to training *daily* so we can keep our skills sharp, develop new skills, and continue to grow.

As soon as you hit the day when you feel you've arrived and don't need to learn more, *mark it on a calendar*. I guarantee, you can look back later and that will be the day you started slipping backwards.

As salespeople are learning new skills on JVTN®, I recommend they *recertify on our core courses at least 2 times every year*.

4. Too Many – Too Soon

Speed kills sales on the lot, speed kills skill development, and if you aren't careful, speed will kill your goals before you know it.

The first step in goal setting is to put your daydreaming hat back on, and start making that *wish* list. My first goal list had over 100 things on it that I wanted or needed.

But if you have a list of 25, 50 or 100 goals you're going to try to achieve in the next 30 days, common sense says you'll miss most of them. It's just too many to focus on at one time.

Because almost all goals depend on skill improvement, it's much better to stick with a single core skill (follow up, closing, negotiating, etc.) so you can spend the time it takes to actually develop and own that particular skill in 30 days.

It's fine to have several goals tied to your skills (sell more, earn more, improve) and to have multiple activities (more demos, write ups) tied to your goals. Just make sure you're actually developing these critical skills, not just watching videos on JVTN®.

5. Rewrite and review your goals, several times a day.

An important component to goal setting is to develop internal buy-in that you really *can* and *will* accomplish your goals – that *'definiteness of purpose'* W.C. Stone talks about.

If you're setting goals to stretch yourself, especially in the beginning, it's common to have a few lingering doubts that pop up on a tough day, even when your goals are realistic.

That's why you want to review your goals as often as possible. With 3 to 5 key goals each month, you want to *rewrite each goal daily,* then read each goal out loud 10 times each day. Why? Because every time you write your goal and say it out loud, you reinforce your internal belief that you'll hit your goal.

> *You'll actually feel your doubts disappear and you'll also feel each doubt slowly being replaced with confidence.*

Tip: If you want to hit your goals faster, *cheat...*

Have your written goals in several places, so you're forced to see them again and again throughout the day. When you're wasting time and about to grab a cup of coffee, if you have your goals on a sticky note stuck to your money, you'll read them.

Keep this simple...

- Write your goals on a sticky note and put one on the refrigerator.

- Put another sticky with your money, so you'll read it each time you reach for your money.

- Code a 12 unit / $4,500 goal as 12-45 and tape it on the back side of your work phone, so you see it several times a day.

- Write your goals on a 3 x 5 card, carry it in your pocket and read it several times each day.

- Put 12 units / $4,500 as a daily reminder in your cell phone.

- Use the VSA® in JVTN® and you'll be reminded of your goal every time you log in and see your progress chart.

- Create a vision board of those pictures we talked about earlier to get your family involved so they remind you, too.

6. Use a daily Journal.

Your mind is a computer and you can literally program your success. Using a journal helps you do that, especially when you fill it out at night. Those positive thoughts rumble around in your head while you sleep to help you find solutions to hit your goals.

Most of the experts I learned from referred to using journals in some form or another. I just ran across my old journals and I can literally read along as I follow my progress. I'm not talking about writing a book, just short, dated entries like...

> 11/17 ... Today was great. I made 6 new contacts, gave 4 excellent presentations and two that were pretty good. I delivered two units today, made $750 and also got a $50 spiff and a $100 pull.
>
> Tomorrow is going to be even better. I'm on track to hit my 30 unit goal, and ahead of my goal to make $17,500 this month. Tomorrow I'll deliver 2 more units, earn over $500 again, and I'll make 10 phone contacts to my sold customers and ask every one of them for referrals. I'll contact everyone who hasn't purchased and I'll meet at least 3 people in Service and use the referral script with them, too. Tomorrow will be AWESOME!

7. Create a Vision Board and make your success a family project.

Want somebody to cheer you on? Do you wish you had somebody in your corner when you're tired and worn out after one of those *ding to dong* days? Well, like we said earlier, your greatest cheerleaders can be your family – especially if they're involved in your goals and in your rewards.

Make your success a family project and create a vision board at home. Just get an inexpensive corkboard and put it somewhere the entire family will see. Put all of your goals on the board, especially your family goals, and use *pictures* so everyone is *seeing* the same vision. Also post and update a progress chart from our Monthly Planning Guide of your success every day.

If a family goal is to get a 3 bedroom house with a white picket fence on a half-acre with a horse stall out back, find a picture of a house closest to what you want, cut out a picture of a horse, (better get a pick-up truck, too), and put them on your board.

If you all want a boat, get a picture and create your income and sales activity goals as your action plan to get the boat. If the family wants to go to Disney World next summer, get pictures of the park, add a picture of the hotel, add some Mickey Mouse ears, and if you really want it to happen, make the total commitment and buy your tickets now.

Important – make sure you put your sales goals next to your family goals, so everyone realizes they can get that house, that boat, or that vacation *as long as you hit your goals at work*.

8. Be careful who you share your goals with.

Everyone wants support. But in real life, if you work with a bunch of friendly but lazy salespeople, you already know that talking about your goals with them will get you every response *but* that high-five you're hoping for.

To reach your goals, only share them with the people you know will support you 100%. Why even bother telling other people? Just set your goals and get to work – they'll find out later!

9. Never arrive!

Personal and professional growth is like taking a never ending journey. You'll have fun, meet a lot of great people and stop at fabulous places along the way.

Don't forget though, that *growth is an ongoing journey* which means these destinations are meant to be *temporary* stopping points. If your goal is to retire at __ (you pick the age) and then to spend the rest of your life __ (you pick what you'll do), that's great. When you arrive, enjoy it – you've earned it!

But until you reach that point, as soon as you stop planning your next goal, wherever you stop becomes your final destination.

Other than your ultimate lifetime goals, always remember whether you're talking personally or professionally...

Growth is a journey – not a destination.

Setting Goals Is A Choice – Not A Requirement

One of the books I read early on was a book called "Choices" by Shad Helmstetter. I didn't like it, because it reminds all of us about the choices we're faced with in life.

Example: When you honestly don't realize you could sell more by doing follow-up, technically you're off the hook about why you aren't selling more cars – you don't know.

But once you understand that more follow-up logically equals more sales and a higher income, then if you choose not to follow-up – you've made a *conscious choice* not to sell more units and not to earn more. *Becoming aware makes it a choice.*

From reading "Choices", I realized that literally *everything* in life and about selling is a choice. You choose to go to work and do your best every day – or you choose to hang around all day and wait for something to happen.

You'll also choose to read my books, attend our classes, train daily on JVTN® and practice every day to become a 30, 40 or 50-car guy – or you'll explain why you don't.

You'll choose to give that next prospect your absolute best presentation – or you'll choose not to. And if you choose not to work smart every day, and choose not to give great presentations to every prospect, then by default, *you've chosen not to increase your sales or your income.*

'Sales' is full of potential and you can accomplish any goal you set and you can earn any amount of money you want to earn. It's really pretty simple – just choose to set clear goals, choose to learn more every day, choose to give it your very best every day at work and you'll earn more, every year.

> *"It's only when you exercise your right to <u>choose</u>, that you can also exercise your right to <u>change</u>!"*
> – *Shad Helmstetter*

Now it's time to get ready to read about the Best Kept Secret in Goal Setting...

When salespeople say,
"But, Joe, I hate tracking..." I really do get it.

The managers in my first dealership didn't teach us anything about anything, but we had to enter everything we did in the log book before we went home. Then they'd use what we'd put in the tracking log to yell at us for doing everything wrong.

We got tired of getting beaten up every day for logging numbers they didn't like, so we told them whatever they wanted to hear. We just put down phony numbers and it worked.

They stopped yelling and we settled in as a bunch of 6 and 8-car guys who had no clue about how to really sell a car, much less how to become successful in sales with tracking and goals.

My managers were wrong, and I was wrong about tracking. When I look back though, I can't blame them – it wasn't their fault. My managers had never been taught how to sell or how to use tracking either, and they only used tracking the way it had been used *on* them, and not *for* them.

I am a hard worker and was always willing to learn. But I wasted my first five years in sales, and they wasted the sales I could have made for the dealership – all because none of us understood tracking or how to use it to set goals to become successful.

So if you really don't like tracking – congratulations – because you're about to learn how to use it to control your success.

CHAPTER 9

TRACKING

THE BEST KEPT SECRET

IN GOAL SETTING

It's a shame tracking has such a bad rap because it's just *counting* things. In fact, it's so simple you only have to count about a half-dozen things each day in sales.

People hear about the *bad,* but not about the *good* and they don't realize tracking is the *foundation* of their future. If you track, you can grow on purpose. If you don't, you have to work hard and hope it all works out.

Tracking really is your secret to success. So let me answer your questions and explain the benefits *to you.* Then let me show you what I've learned about how to use tracking to *set clear result and activity goals* that *guarantee* your growth, year after year.

"Why do I need to track things, Joe?
I pretty much know what's going on..."

Just like athletes in every sport, like every major business, and all of those 3%'ers in sales – it's simple – you track (count) everything you do, so you can *immediately* spot both your problems and opportunities.

Why does it matter? Well, if you *think* you're selling more than you are and set what you feel is a reasonable goal based on that *guesstimate,* if your starting point is *too high,* your goal will end up being *unrealistic.*

The reverse is true, too. If you *think* you're selling less than you are and set a realistic goal from that *guesstimate,* your goal will be *too low.*

The key to tracking is to find your *90-day current averages,* then learn how to use your averages to set accurate goals.

A quick example ... Don't look up any of your sales history, just follow this first step right now, before you keep reading:

1. Start at Month 1, which is 12 months ago, and fill in the blanks in column 'A' on how many sales *you think* you made each month. Then after you've entered all of your guesstimates, add those all together to *find your total guesstimates for the last 12 months.*

    Don't do anything else, just fill in your guesstimates and total...

Month	A. Guesstimate	B. Actual	C. _____
1.	_____	_____	(We'll cover 'C'
2.	_____	_____	in a later chapter.)
3.	_____	_____	_____
4.	_____	_____	_____
5.	_____	_____	_____
6.	_____	_____	_____
7.	_____	_____	_____
8.	_____	_____	_____
9.	_____	_____	
10.	_____	_____	_____
11.	_____	_____	_____
Last mo.	_____	_____	_____
Total	_____	_____	

Do not continue until you've completed column A.

2. Only *after* you've filled in your last 12 month guesstimates and totaled those, pull out your sales records and write in your *actual sales* for those 12 months and total those, too, in column 'B', Actual.

   Complete column 'B' before you go any further.

   After you filled out 'B', was your sales guesstimate
   in 'A' exact, was it higher or was it lower than your actual?

   ❏ Exact   ❏ Higher   ❏ Lower

3. Now starting with 12 months ago *first,* in the blank chart put a dot by your *actual* sales each month, then connect the dots. When you're done, it will look something like the sample chart.

Once you've
added the dots
and connected
them, you'll see a
picture of *where
you've been* in
sales and *where
you're headed.*

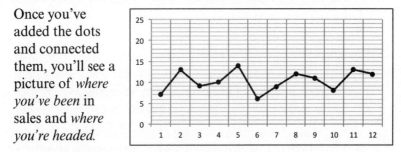

Fill in this blank chart with your 'Actual' sales history from 'B'.

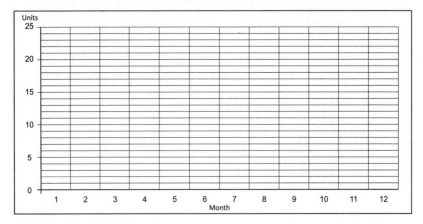

How did your guesstimates compare with your actual sales?
What do you *see* in your chart? Are you headed up, down or both?

"What areas should I be tracking?"
The easy answer ... everything!

1. **Track all of your <u> opportunities </u> to make a sale.**

   You want to count every person you talk to; people on the lot, incoming sales calls, and web leads. Why? To set an improvement goal, you need to find your *actual* closing (delivery) ratio of how many you deliver versus how many you *really* talk to.

   Your opportunities would include...

   ✓ Traffic on the lot right now, from any source.

   On your floor traffic, you also want to track each opportunity by the *type* of prospect they are: Walk-in, repeat, referral, sales call, internet lead, be-back, etc.

   Why? Because you're probably spending 90% of your time with the toughest to close prospects (walk-ins). You want to start working with the *easiest* and most productive prospects, *so you can double your sales and income and go home on time.*

   - **Walk-Ins ...** The *real* average closing ratio for a pure ad-driven or drive-by walk-in customer is about 10% and the gross (commission) on this group is the lowest of any group because most are (price) shoppers.

   - **Repeat Customers ...** The *real* average closing ratio for a repeat customer is about 70% and the average gross profit is 40% higher. Why? Because they like you, and because they are *rarely* active price shoppers.

   - **Referrals from Prospecting ...** Referrals are almost the same as repeat customers: 60-70% + 40% higher gross.

   - **Be-Backs ...** The closing ratio when you get a customer who left back on the lot: 67%. The gross will depend on whether you've focused on value or price.

   - **Incoming Calls / Internet Leads ...** Closing ratio on the phone: 0% ... but 50% of these buy when they do come into the dealership. The gross with each depends on whether you focused on value or price to get them in.

✓ Incoming Sales Calls.

The only goal on this call is to turn this prospect into an appointment that shows up on the lot asking for you. Count...

- # of incoming sales calls you get
- # of appointments you set from these calls
- # of appointments that show up asking for you

✓ Incoming calls from your own previous customers, referrals or friends about a vehicle. The only goal on this call is also to turn each call into an appointment that will show up asking for you. Count...

- # of calls you get
- # of appointments you set from these contacts
- # of appointments that show up asking for you

✓ Internet Leads / Web Leads (all types). The goal is exactly the same – turn each lead into an appointment that shows up on the lot asking for you. Count...

- # of leads you get
- # of appointments you set from these leads
- # of appointments that show up asking for you

☞ Tip On Internet Leads: Instead of sending ten emails back and forth, just pick up the phone and call them at the number they gave you on the lead.

How do you keep track of all of these people?

That's easy, if you're using our Weekly Pocket Guide. Enter their name and contact info, and enter the *count* in the weekly summary.

At the end of the day or end of the week, just transfer everything that happened today or this week, into your VSA® in JVTN®.

After that, your Virtual Sales Assistant® (VSA®) will do all of the heavy lifting with your contacts, call back reminders and ongoing follow up, and it will take care of all the tracking, averaging, charting *and* give you the projections you need to set your goals.

2. **Track all of your lead generation ___activities___ .**

The secret (and shortcut) to becoming a high achiever is to stop waiting for your dealer to supply you with those tough to close walk-in prospects. Instead, set clear goals to make sure you have people walking in the door asking for you *every single day*.

☞ *All of the people who ask for you will be five times easier to close and will pay 40% more in gross profit (commission).*

Why? Because 71% of the people say they buy from people they like and trust. That's why repeat business and referrals are so much easier to work with (70% closing ratio) compared to that walk-in stranger at just 10%, who doesn't like you or know you.

Lead generation activities are all of the things *you personally do* each day to generate more of your own traffic. Count...

✓ Your outbound prospecting calls each day to your previous customers, acquaintances, orphan owners in the dealership and Parts & Service customers.

Remember the goal – schedule a firm appointment that will show up asking for you. Count...

-   # of calls you make each day
-   # of appointments you set from your outbound calls
-   # of appointments that show up asking for you

✓ Your in-person Service prospecting contacts each day.

30% of the customers on your Service Drive each day have a family member who will be buying a vehicle within the next 90 days. Your goal – using the referral script, find that next buyer in the family and get them in for an appointment.

Also, when you're back in Service and you get any interest, bring them up front and follow every step in the selling process.

-   # of contacts you make each day
-   # of appointments you set from these contacts
-   # of appointments that show or that you bring up front

✓ Your unsold follow up contacts, to get them back in.

It's important to understand the value of this group. 78% were buyers when they walked on the lot, which means 78% are still buyers. And like a repeat or referral customer, they come back partially because they like you. The closing ratio with this group (be-backs) is 67% on that second visit. So count...

- # of calls you make each day to your unsold customers
- # of texts and emails you send each day
- # of appointments you set from those contacts
- # of appointments that come back in asking for you

✓ Your sold customer follow up and retention contacts.

This is your target group of customers to guarantee your long-term success and continued growth in sales.

95% will buy more vehicles. As a family, they'll purchase a total of 36 vehicles. With effective follow up and with a long-term retention plan, you can capture 75% as *forever* customers.

Growth is automatic and guaranteed when you make retaining each customer your top priority. Back to our growth at JVG for a second – we grow over 50% per year, but we cheat.

We take care of our customers so well, and we support our online training so well, that over 90% of our business each year comes from repeat and referral customers. We still have many of our original customers today, 27 years later.

You can learn how to do the same thing, and it starts with a continuous follow up and retention process. Count...

- # of calls you make each day to your sold customers
- # of emails you send to this group each day
- # of appointments you set from these contacts
- # of appointments that show up asking for you

Lead generation is critical to your consistent growth. It's how you flood the floor every day with customers asking for you.

3. **Track your selling ___activities___.**

    Selling *activities* are all of the things you do once you're in front of a customer to actually make a sale. Count...

    ✓ # demonstrations you give each day

    ✓ # uncommitted write ups you get each day

    ✓ # fully committed write ups you get each day

    Why count write ups *two ways?* Because with uncommitted people, you're usually closing on price. That guarantees a tougher sale, with lower gross. When people are fully committed, it's more about the vehicle, the features and benefits, than price.

    By tracking your write ups both ways, one of your goals will be to learn how to get more real commitments, and I don't mean twisting arms or making them sign something that says, "If the terms and figures are agreeable, we will buy today."

    Go through the courses on selling, price, closing, handling objections and negotiation on JVTN® and learn how to get the firmest commitments you've ever gotten – all without ever directly asking the customer to buy.

4. **Track all of your ___results___ in sales.**

    These are the end results of all of your opportunities and your lead generation and selling activities. Count...

    ✓ Your deliveries

    ✓ Your commissions

    ✓ Bonuses, spiffs, factory cash, gas ticket, coffee coupon, etc.

    Selling really is about the numbers.

Tracking is just numbers. It's simply counting everything you do. Once you have this information, and learn to *see* what the numbers mean – and once you learn how to use this information correctly (we'll cover that next), the sky is the limit on your improvement.

CHAPTER 10

THE EASY WAY TO TRACK
EVERYTHING YOU DO

OK – you have a better understanding of *why* you
need to track what you do, and we've talked about
what things you need to track.

Now let's learn *how* to quickly gather this information,
so you can start using it to help you control your sales
and income each month, and see how tracking helps
you grow, year after year.

Let's start with the easy steps to tracking all of your
opportunities, activities and results. Then we'll talk
about how to find your *current averages* to use as your
baseline for almost all of your results, your activity
improvements and your growth goals.

What are the steps to tracking?

What do you really have to track and how long does it take?

Keep it simple...

1. <u>Count</u> every opportunity, activity and result each day.

2. <u>Log</u> every opportunity, activity and result you count.

3. <u>Average</u> every opportunity, activity and result you log.

4. Use your current averages and projections to <u>set your goals</u>.

What should you count?

Using these abbreviations as a guide, enter your #s of each into the Weekly Summary in your WPG, MPG, or directly into your VSA®.

Opportunities...

  # UPs .... Walk-in traffic

  # PH Show .... Incoming sales calls that show

  # IP Show...... Internet / Web prospects that show for their appointment

  # OP.............. Outside prospects you bring on the lot

  # DC .... Dealership customers (from all departments)

  # RP.............. Repeat customers

  # RF.............. Referrals

  # BB.............. The Be-Backs you bring back in, who didn't buy before

  # TR.............. The turns you take or give

Activities...

  # Demos

  # Write Ups

  # Outgoing Prospecting, Follow Up calls you make

  # Mail / Emails / Texts

Results...

  # Deliveries

  $ Earned

Incoming Calls & Internet Lead Activities...

  # Calls / Internet leads

  # Appointments you set

  # Appointments that show

  # Sales / Deliveries

What are the steps to tracking?

With our Weekly Pocket Guide (WPG, below) or our Monthly Planning Guide (MPG, on the next page) tracking is really a non-event.

It takes seconds to enter your numbers into the WPG. Carrying it with you will save time, it will remind you of every step of the sale, and prompt you to get all of the contact info you need to follow up.

Time Required: Seconds Per Day.

I wish I could say it was tough to track what happens every day in sales. I know it would sure make most salespeople feel a lot better about not keeping up with everything they do, so they can set clear goals in sales and continually improve their income.

WEEKLY SUMMARY					From: _/_ To: _/_				
Day	1	2	3	4	5	6	7	TTL
Opportunities									
#UP	2	__	__	__	__	__	__	__
#PH Show	1	__	__	__	__	__	__	__
#IP Show	__	__	__	__	__	__	__	__
#OP	__	__	__	__	__	__	__	__
#DC	1	__	__	__	__	__	__	__
#RP	__	__	__	__	__	__	__	__
#RF	__	__	__	__	__	__	__	__
#BB	1	__	__	__	__	__	__	__
#TR	__	__	__	__	__	__	__	__
Total	5	__	__	__	__	__	__	__
Activities									
#Demos	4	__	__	__	__	__	__	__
#Write-Ups	3	__	__	__	__	__	__	__
#Out Calls	8	__	__	__	__	__	__	__
#Mail / Emails	2	__	__	__	__	__	__	__
Results									
#Delivered	2	__	__	__	__	__	__	__
$Earned	$753	__	__	__	__	__	__	__

Incoming Call / Internet Lead Activities

#Calls / Int.	C/I	2/C_	_/_	_/_	_/_	_/_	_/_	_/_
#Appts	C/I	1/C_	_/_	_/_	_/_	_/_	_/_	_/_
#Shows	C/I	1/C_	_/_	_/_	_/_	_/_	_/_	_/_
#Sales	C/I	1/C_	_/_	_/_	_/_	_/_	_/_	_/_

Don't even let yourself think this is hard. Once you have the numbers, just...

✓ Log what you do each day in our Weekly or Monthly Planner.

✓ Enter your info into the VSA® on JVTN® and it will take care of the averaging, charting and projections you need.

✓ Based on your current averages and projections, you'll then have a base to set clear goals and create an effective plan of action.

✓ Because you're tracking everything, you'll know *exactly* what activities to focus on for your Action Plan.

The Monthly Planning Guide (MPG)

Transfer your daily information from your Weekly Pocket Guide to the MPG if you don't have JVTN®. Or enter it directly into the VSA®, where everything is tracked and averaged automatically.

Use The VSA® For Tracking & Goals

If you're using the VSA®, enter all of your daily information and the VSA® will take care of the averaging and charting. You'll use that information to set your goals at the beginning of each month.

**When you can *see* what you're doing,
setting clear goals to improve is so much easier.**

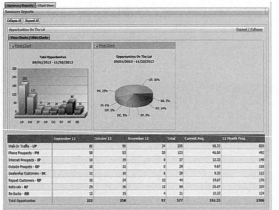

Track your floor traffic to see where your best selling opportunities are coming from.

Track your incoming leads and outgoing prospecting to see what's working to drive more traffic.

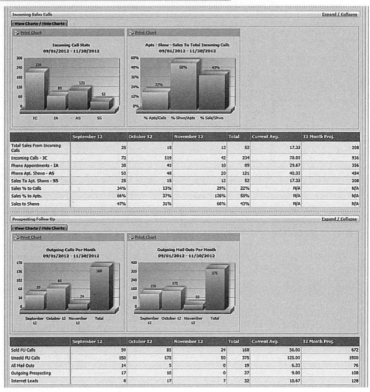

CHAPTER 11

CURRENT AVERAGES

WHAT THEY ARE & WHY YOU NEED THEM

My first dealership kept all of their yearly sales books, and if it was July 1st, they'd look at last July, and the July before that and try to figure out the goal for this July. If we were averaging 125 units, but the last few Julys we sold 75, they'd actually set a goal under 100, just because that's what we did a few years ago.

There are so many examples that prove this method was incredibly ineffective. There's way too much old stuff using a 6 or 12-month average, much less relying on 3 or 4-year old sales information.

To start controlling your career – stop looking so far backwards, and instead just focus everything on your *current 90-day average*. That's the only number you need to know to continually improve, year after year.

Why Use Current Averages?

A current average is your most recent 3 month average.

Example: You sold 8 (3 mo. ago) + 10 (2 mo. ago) + 12 (last mo.) = 30.

Now divide your 3 month total sales (30) by 3 and that means your *current 90-day average* is 10 units per month.

But why focus just on the last three months?

Because 2 months isn't long enough, and anything older than a 3 months will be a distorted average, compared to what's really going on right now, today, in your career. To plan your growth *tomorrow,* you have to start with what you're doing *now,* and the only 'now' average you want to look at is your current 90-day average.

You need these current averages for several reasons in goal setting...

☞ **Forecasting Is Based On Your Current Averages**

Forecasting tells you what you'll ___probably get___ if you keep doing what you're doing, and external influences stay the same.

A forecast is based on your current average in a specific area like units, gross, repeat business, etc. Example: If you've sold 14 units every month for the last 3 months, and you just keep doing what you're doing, you'll probably sell 14 units next month.

6 months ago	8
5 months ago	8
4 months ago	8
3 months ago	14
2 months ago	14
last month	14

Without even doing the math above, it's pretty obvious you're forecasted to have another 14-unit month because that's what you're doing *lately*. It wouldn't make sense to average all six months and use an 11-unit average to set a goal for next month.

Most of the time, it isn't quite as easy to see what's going on. That's why you need to track everything you do to get your current averages. To set goals, you want to start with an accurate forecast.

☞ **Projections Are Based On Your Current Averages (Forecasts)**

Projections take forecasting a step further by also taking into account all of the _stuff_ that can affect your forecast.

Normal things come up every month like a shorter or longer month, a vacation, a special event sale, 5 weekends or anything else that can affect your sales volume in any given month.

Example: If you're taking a 7-day vacation, unless you do some extra activities the other three weeks, your forecast needs to be adjusted for the lost time and lost selling activities next month.

Here's something most people don't take into account...

Being off a week, you can and should put in extra time the three weeks you're at work to keep this from costing you 25% of your volume and income. But missing a week this month normally affects the *following* month more than the *current* month.

Why? Because results lag a week or two behind *activities.* You may close more deals in those three weeks, *but you won't be doing* as much prospecting, or follow up, or getting incoming calls or Internet leads *for seven days.* So unless you pound the phones (activities) those three weeks you're there to make sure you have appointments and deals working *next month,* that's when you'll likely take the biggest hit from your time off.

☞ **Goals Are Based On Your Current Averages & Projections**

Goals are what you _want to happen_ instead of your projections.

You forecast to see what will *probably* happen, then you factor in the *stuff,* so you can make a more accurate projection. Then you set your improvement goals based on your final projections.

☞ **'Activity Action Plans' Are Also Based On Your Current Averages**

Taking *action* is where you __make it happen__.

Goals don't make things happen, they're just your target. Now it's time to develop your *Activity Action Plan* and spell out exactly what you'll need to do to reach each of your goals.

*"But I'm still not convinced to use my 90-day current average
as the starting point instead of my annual average, tell me more..."*

That's OK, I understand. Here's another common example:

Here are sales for two different salespeople, the first six months of
the year. Let's see how their averages look if we figure this both ways;
a six-month average versus just their last 90-day current average.

Salesperson #1 started our training and got better.

Salesperson #2 stopped our training.

First, find each salesperson's *6-month average.*

Next, find each salesperson's *90-day current average.*

Salesperson #1		Salesperson #2	
Jan	9	Jan	22
Feb	10	Feb	20
Mar	11	Mar	18
Apr	18	Apr	11
May	20	May	10
Jun	22	Jun	9
Total	**90**	**Total**	**90**

A. 6-Mo. Average ____
B. Current Average ____
(April, May, June)

A. 6-Mo. Average ____
B. Current Average ____
(April, May, June)

If you're trying to set a realistic goal for the next month, which
average (A or B) makes the most sense to use as your guide? Which
gives you the best indication of what this salesperson is doing *now?*

- ❑ A: The six-month average is the best indicator of what is going
  on now and what the salesperson will most likely do next.

- ❑ B: The current average is the best indicator of what is going
  on now and what the salesperson will most likely do next.

Let's do some easy forecasting and projections for goal setting...

It's important you understand *why* you use *current averages (forecasting)* as your base for projections, why you need forecasting *and* projections, and then how to use both to set *realistic goals*.

- ✓ Your Current Average is *where you are now* in unit sales (unit sales is what we're tracking in our example). Your *forecast (current average) is your base* for projections.

- ✓ Projections *start with your current average* <u>and</u> also take everything else into consideration that could affect your sales next month. Projections are what you *expect to happen.*

- ✓ Goal Setting is what you *want to happen.* Based on your forecast and projections, you'll set a realistic improvement goal.

- ✓ Last you'll create an Activity Action Plan. This is your written plan on exactly what you will do to *hit your goal.*

Four Quick Examples

Let's look at four more quick examples of averaging (forecasting) and projections so you understand how to figure all of this out and set more effective goals for improvement.

1. Find this salesperson's *Current Average* and *July Projections...*

Month	Jan	Feb	Mar	Apr	May	Jun	Cur. Avg.	July Projection
Units	8	8	8	8	8	8	_____	_____

That was easy, and here's how this salesperson's sales look in a chart: Flat line.

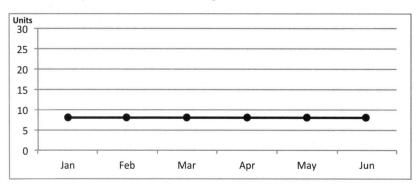

2. Let's try a common example of inconsistency...

Month	Jan	Feb	Mar	Apr	May	Jun	Cur. Avg.	July Projection
Units	8	14	8	14	8	14	_____	_____

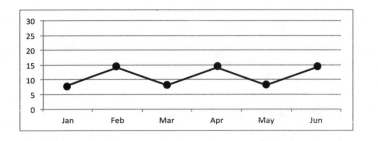

3. How about if the dealership had a big event in June...

Month	Jan	Feb	Mar	Apr	May	Jun	Cur. Avg.	July Projection
Units	8	8	8	8	8	29	_____	_____

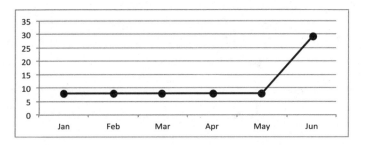

4. Or how about after a March Madness weekend blow out...

Month	Jan	Feb	Mar	Apr	May	Jun	Cur. Avg.	July Projection
Units	8	8	18	8	8	8	_____	_____

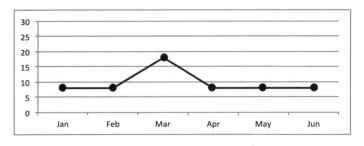

The projection in all four examples is 8 units.

The July projection is 8 units in each example, even though in #2, 3 and 4 it isn't based *just* on the current average forecast.

In #1, it's evident. This is a flat line 8-car guy who doesn't fluctuate.

In #2, even though he has a 14-car month every other month and his current average is actually 12, he *consistently* has an 8-car month every other month. Unfortunately, July falls on an 8-unit month.

In #3, there was a special event that boosted his sales. He's still an 8-car guy – not a 15-car guy (current average) just because he had a great month. In fact, he'll probably have a 4 or 5-car month in July from the 'afterglow' of extra units and extra cash in his pocket.

In #4, that good month back in March is now history. He was and still is just an 8-car guy who had a good month and 8 units is exactly what he can expect next month, unless something *extra* happens.

Current averages are your baseline forecasting tool.
Projections start with your baseline and go from there.

Current averages are a *guide* to what will probably happen, but you can't just use that average. You also need to take everything else into consideration (projections) before you set your goals.

How about you?

We've talked about averages and making projections so you can set clear goals. So that you can be prepared, list what you think could affect your projections next month...

_____	_____	_____
_____	_____	_____
_____	_____	_____

Now start thinking about how you can *make up* for any lost time or other situations that could *cost* you sales, or how you can *take advantage* of any longer months, special events or extra inventory.

When you prepare ahead of time,
you can have a great month, every month.

Stop Here!

If you haven't already, it's time to find your 90-day current average, so you can create accurate projections.

1. Go back to page 58 of 'Tracking' where you originally did your *guesstimates* and your *actual* sales for the year.

2. Now in column 'C' on page 58, find your current averages.

    It takes 3 months to get a current average and that's why the first blank line under current average starts in month 3.

    Just take the 3 month average of months 1, 2 & 3, and enter that in the first current average blank in month 3.

    That's your *current* average for the first 3 months.

    When you use a current 90-day average, *you will drop your oldest month, each month.* So in the next blank, find your current average of months 2, 3 & 4 and enter that in month 4.

    Do the same, and fill in all of the current average blanks.

3. Next, using a thicker line or a different color pen, chart your *90-day current average* each month in the chart you completed on page 59. Just start in month 3, put a dot for the current average each month, and then just connect your dots.

    Charting your monthly sales *sort of* gives you a picture of where you're headed, but as you've seen, when you only look at the monthly number in a chart, sometimes it's hard to get the best picture on where you're actually headed.

    By also charting your current average, you'll notice it doesn't have those big swings that charting your units has. Your current average chart shows you exactly where you're headed.

    Your goal now is to start *managing your current average*.

*For continuous growth,
focus on continually improving
your current average.*

CHAPTER 12

A Picture Is Worth
Way More Than 1,000 Words

When I started tracking, I realized I'd better learn how to use a computer to help me. Now I have dozens of spreadsheets that track everything we do at work.

My problem with all of those spreadsheets is that like most people, I don't assimilate rows of numbers very well, it's too hard. But we're all good with pictures.

So instead of just sheet after sheet with row after row of numbers, I rely on charts to *show me* what most of those numbers mean. That's why we've included so many charts in JVTN® and the VSA® – so you can *see* what you're doing and where you're headed in each area.

Let's look at a few examples of the different types of charts you can use to more clearly *see* the different numbers you want to start managing and improving.

A Picture Is Worth A Thousand Words

*Different types of charts
show you different types of information.*

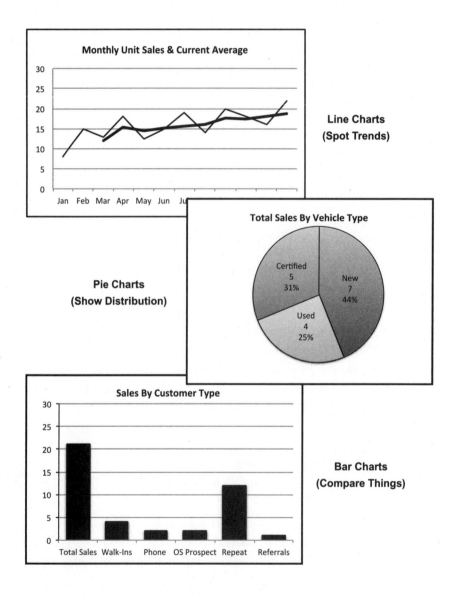

Monthly Unit Sales & Current Average

**Line Charts
(Spot Trends)**

**Pie Charts
(Show Distribution)**

Total Sales By Vehicle Type

Certified
5
31%

New
7
44%

Used
4
25%

Sales By Customer Type

**Bar Charts
(Compare Things)**

Total Sales Walk-Ins Phone OS Prospect Repeat Referrals

Example: Use charts to help you focus on your best prospects.

The charts below look at a breakdown by % of sales by customer type (walk-in / repeat / etc.) and commission by customer type.

1. Take a minute to look at them. What do you <u>see</u> in these two charts: Sales by customer type and commission by customer type?

2. Which type of customer does this salesperson primarily sell to?

    _____

3. Which type earned him the highest commissions? _____

4. Even without selling more, he could make more money selling the same number of cars by focusing on which groups? _____

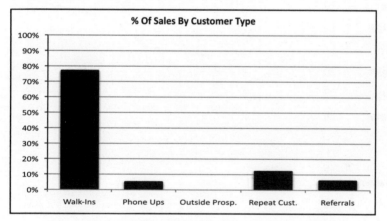

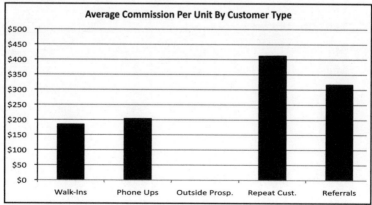

Salesperson #1 and Salesperson #2

Do you remember how close they looked when you only saw their numbers? Especially since they'd both sold 90 units so far this year.

Notice how your vision changes *immediately* when you *see a chart* of those two salespeople who have identical unit totals for the year, instead of just looking at their numbers...

What do you <u>clearly</u> see now?

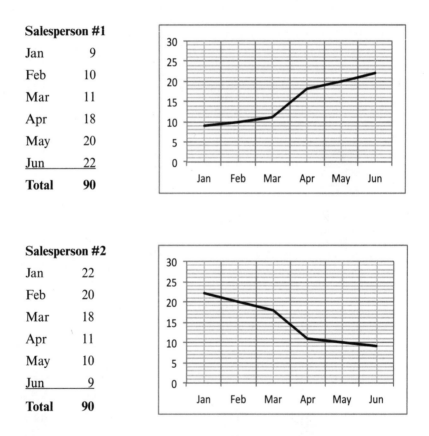

Salesperson #1	
Jan	9
Feb	10
Mar	11
Apr	18
May	20
Jun	22
Total	**90**

Salesperson #2	
Jan	22
Feb	20
Mar	18
Apr	11
May	10
Jun	9
Total	**90**

Both salespeople have exactly the same sales volume, but each of them is headed in a completely different direction!

Key Words To Remember In Career Management...

- Initial Training

- Tracking

- Current Averaging / Forecasting

- Charting

- Projecting

- Setting Goals

- Activity Planning

- Skill Development

- Determination

- Confidence

- Self-Discipline

- Continuing Education

Does tracking, averaging, charting and goal setting really work?

At Joe Verde Sales & Management Training, Inc., our ongoing business goal is to grow. To do that, we focus all of our goals on improving our training, our products, our processes and most important, our ongoing training support for our customers.

To improve in these areas, we rely on our tracking to improve our current averages in the relevant *activities* to make it happen. From our daily tracking and our short, medium, and long-term goals, we improve *something* we do, every single day.

In our 27 years in business, we've had 24 record years, and we've averaged a 53% improvement <u>every</u> year. *So, "Yes, it works!"*

Here's a salesperson who fell for what we teach about developing his skills and setting clear goals.

"I tripled my take home pay after reading Joe's book!"

"Before reading your book 'How To Sell A Car Today' I was selling 8-9 units a month and bringing home about $3,500.

I've read it three times in the past couple of months and now, selling is simple: I present the features and benefits Joe's way and handle objections on the lot. When it comes time to close, assuming the sale now just comes natural. Last month I more than tripled my pay check and took home $12,000!"

– Jim, Salesperson, Ford, Georgia

CHAPTER 13

UNDERSTANDING HOW TO
CONTROL YOUR CURRENT AVERAGE

You can't control everything that happens in sales every month, but you can almost completely control your current average *by controlling your activities*, which in turn will give you control of your sales and income.

My personal goal in sales every month is to keep our current average moving higher in everything we do, and that should be your new goal, too.

Find your current averages in units, gross, income, CSI, repeat business, referrals, demos, write ups, appointments you set and appointments that show, prospecting calls, follow up calls, and the other positive opportunities, activities and results we've listed in this book. Then just improve your current averages in those areas, and more sales and income will follow.

To Set Clear Goals To Raise Your Current Average
You Have To Understand The Math

Easy Math ... A current average is a 3-month average. If you want to average 12 units, how many do you need to sell in that 90-day period?

Correct, you'll need to sell 36 units in 90 days.

OK – let's assume these are your last three months' sales....

    8 three months ago

   10 two months ago

  <u> 12</u> last month

   30 total, for a 10-unit current average

How do you raise your current average from 10 to 12 units?

This month, you want to raise your current average from 10 to 12 units. That seems like a realistic goal. So how many units do you need to sell this month to raise you current average to 12?

The Math ... There are a couple of ways to do the math, but since you have a *current average goal* (3-month average), I personally like to just multiply your *current average goal* (12) by 3, so you know how many *total* units you'll need to sell in this 3-month period.

    3 months

 <u>x 12</u> average

   36 total units you need to sell in this three-month period

You have 2 months of the 3 months to count, so just *subtract your last two months' sales* to find your unit goal for this month.

The 3rd month back, the 8-unit month, drops off. You sold 10 units two months ago and 12 units last month. Just subtract the total of those (22) from the total you need to sell in this 3 month period.

   36 total needed in 3 months

 <u>– 22</u> (10 + 12) you already sold the last 2 months

   14 is your goal this month to raise your average to 12

Here's something most salespeople don't realize...

Depending on the month that's dropping off, sometimes your actual goal to raise your current average could be lower than your average, and sometimes it could be higher. So let's do two more problems, and I'll show you what I mean.

Goal # 1: Raise your average to 16 units.
3 months ago you sold 20, 2 months ago 15, last month 10.
That's 45 units total, for a 15-unit current average.

1. The goal is to raise your current average to 16, so how many total units do you need to sell in three months? ____ (3 x 16)

2. You sold 15 two months ago + 10 last month, so that's _25_ of the 48 you need. How many do you need to sell this month? ____

(Yes, your goal can go way up when you drop a big month.)

Goal # 2: Same goal: 16 units, but reverse your sales the last 3 months.
3 months ago you sold 10, 2 months ago 15, last month 20.
That's also 45 units total, for a 15-unit current average.

1. The goal is to raise the current average to 16, so how many total units do you need to sell in 3 months? ____ (3 x 16)

2. You sold 15 two months ago + 20 last month, so that's ____ of the 48 you need. How many do you need to sell this month? ____

When you're working on your current averages,
the goal isn't always what you'd think it would be.

Sometimes your goal is higher than your average, sometimes it's lower. That's why you want to start managing your months better, so you're more consistent and stable in your units and income.

When you start tracking, start setting goals to raise your average and start managing your activities – within 3 months, you'll *stabilize* your sales and eliminate those wild swings. *Then you can really start to grow.*

The A–B–Cs Of Setting Current Average Income Goals

Example of a current average goal for <u>monthly income</u>.
Go slow. This isn't hard, it's just money, instead of units.

A. First, find your current average:

Last month, I earned:	$2,200
Two months ago, I earned:	$1,800
Three months ago, I earned:	<u>$2,000</u>
My three month total:	$6,000
My current average is ($6,000 ÷ 3):	$2,000 per month

B. Next, set a long-term goal and then break it down into medium and short-term goals.

Your Goal: In this example, your *results* goal is to raise your current average income per month from $2,000 now – to $4,000 *in one year*.

----

1 year goal: I will average $4,000 a month, one year from today (add the date).

6 months: I will average $3,000 a month, 6 months from today ($3,000 is halfway from $2,000, *where you are now,* to your $4,000 *one-year* goal.)

3 months: I will average $2,500 a mo. 3 mo. from today. ($2,500 is halfway to your 6 mo. goal of $3,000.)

1 month: I will average $2,167 a month, one month from today (add the date). ($2,167 is one-third of the way to your 3 month goal.)

This Month: **To raise my average to $2,167, this month I will earn $2,500.** See C(3) next page, for the math.

Doubling your income seems huge, but break it down – you just need to raise your average $167 each month. That seems *very* realistic.

C. Now find your goal this month to raise your average to $2,167.

To do that, you need to find out how much you'll have to earn to raise your current average from $2,000 to $2,167.

Find your goal for this month...

(1) Multiply your current average goal for this month.

     $2,167   The goal ($2,166.66 rounded up)

     <u>   x 3</u>   To find the total needed this month

     $6,500   To be earned in this 3-month period

(2) Add your *previous 2 months'* earnings together.

     $1,800   Two months ago

     <u>$2,200</u>   Last month

     $4,000   Total earned in the previous two months

(3) Subtract your last two months' earnings from the total and you'll have your goal for this month that will bring your average to $2,167.

     $6,500   Total needed

   <u>– $4,000</u>   Last two months' earnings

     $2,500   Earnings goal this month

I hope you're starting to see just how easy it can be to manage your unit sales and income to guarantee your growth every month and every year. It's all about managing your current average.

Step One: Stabilizing

Again, your first goal is to stabilize your sales (and income), which you can easily do in three months. Then, once you stop the wild fluctuations, managing everything you do gets easier and easier.

How About Activity Goals?

You calculated your unit and income goals, now it's time to do the same thing with your *activities,* so you know exactly what you need to do to hit your *income* goal in C(3), on the previous page.

1. **First, assume you've tracked to find your averages in these areas.**

    Example of your current averages:

    Avg. # of Opportunities   __50__   (Average # you talk to on the lot)

    Avg. Units Per Month   __10__   (Average # deliveries per month)

    Avg. Commission Per Unit   __$200__ @ 25% commission on $800 gross

    # of Demonstrations   __35__ = __70%__ Demos of 50 Oppts.

    # of Write Ups   __22__ = __63%__ Write Ups of Demos

    # of Deliveries (above)   __10__ = __45%__ Deliveries of Write Ups

    Closing Ratios: 10 of 50 Opportunities   = __20%__ Of all Opportunities

                     10 of 35 Demos   = __28%__ Delivery of Demos

                     10 of 22 Write Ups   = __45%__ Delivery of Write-Ups

2. **Using your current averages above, there are several ways to reach your goal by adjusting your activities.**

    To reach your goal of $2,500 you can...

    A. Sell 12.5 units ($200 per unit x 12.5 = $2,500)

    Based on your closing ratios, you can sell 12.5 units if you:

    a. Talk to 62.5 people instead of 50   (20% Closing Ratio)

    b. Or... give 45 demos instead of 35   (28% of 45 = 12.6)

    c. Or... write up 28 people instead of 22   (45% of 28 people)

    d. Or... improve your closing ratio to 25%   (25% of 50 = 12.5)

B. You could also hit your $2,500 goal without increasing your sales.

How? Just raise your commission to $250 per unit.

If you're paid 25% of the gross profit, you need to raise the gross profit by $200 per unit. You can easily do that...

a. On JVTN® or in our class, learn how to *bypass price* so you can *build value,* instead of getting stuck in a negotiation on the lot, which forces you to give up gross for no reason.

b. On JVTN® or in our classes, learn how to deliver 5 of the 10 units you average to repeat or referral customers from your own prospecting. On average, repeat and referral customers will pay $400 more in gross profit.

$400 per unit extra on 5 of your 10 sales = $2,000.

At 25% commission, that's $500 in total extra income.

c. Learn how to set up the negotiation properly on JVTN® or in class. Negotiating doesn't mean splitting things, but that's what most of us were taught. *Negotiation is a process.* 'Splitting things' just means you leave a ton of gross on the table and miss easy sales every month you could have had.

C. Or you can increase your income with many other combinations.

The point is – once you really track and know all about *who* you talk to, *what* you do each day, and then all of your *averages* on your sales, gross and commissions – you can mix and match half a dozen different ways to increase your current average in units and income, anytime you want to.

I hope you're beginning to realize you can definitely increase your units and your income in several different ways, none of which include working bell to bell, 7 days a week. The only catch is, you have to know your averages and set clear goals to improve.

Tracking is the secret to setting
and reaching your improvement goals.

There really are a lot of very high achievers in sales who started right where you are now. Thousands of salespeople grow and improve once they take our classes and our online courses on JVTN® to learn how to sell on a professional level, and then set clear goals to improve...

- A saleswoman went from 26 to 42 units per month after class, and only works 8-5, Monday through Fridays.
- "After your Sales Course, I went from 10 to 21 units."
- "I'm up to 15 units per month, my commission is up from $416 per unit to $766 and I'm on track to earn $150,000 in the next 12 months."
- "After your sales course, my salesperson went from 7 to 21.5. Not bad for a guy who worked at a fast food place a few months ago."
- A salesperson who averaged about 55 units per month was back in class *again* the month he came off a 96 car month.
- A top Ford salesperson is averaging 40+ units per month.
- This salesperson emailed us that he started our training when he was earning $100,000+. The next year he hit the low $200,000s, then the high $200,000's, the next year over $300,000. His fourth year training, he and his manager called to tell us he earned $455,000.
- A dealer asked me to call his salesperson who earned over $400,000 after our training. He was selling only used vehicles, in a town of 15,000 people *without taking any walk-in traffic.*
- Another salesperson sent me an email..."I earned $1,444,000 selling cars in 4.5 years using the Verde System." (That's $320,888 per year.)

These results are from salespeople who are both brand new and who have been selling cars for years. They all took our training, decided to make the change and became High Achievers In Sales.

If they can get those improvements, so can you.
Set your goals today and get to class and on JVTN®!

To become a Pro – count like a Pro.

Average salespeople count how often things *don't work,* like demos or prospecting calls, to justify why they don't do it.

Pros count how often things *do work,* so they know how many demos or calls it takes to sell more units and earn more money.

Think like a Pro – The sky is the limit.

CHAPTER 14

DIFFERENT GOALS YOU SHOULD CONSIDER SETTING

Everybody is different, so other than the basic goals we've talked about for sales, income, skills, activities and goals to control your sales and income by focusing on your repeat and referral business, there really isn't a set list of all of the different types of goals you need to set or may want to set.

This chapter is a *working* chapter for you to make some decisions on the types of goals you want to set for yourself and your family.

If you're a dealer or manager, take all of the same thoughts in this book and just apply them to your team or your dealership.

Read this chapter when you have some time to yourself.

What's Your Vision?
What Do You Want To Accomplish?

One of the best ways to set clear, short-term goals is to start with the Big Picture. That's pretty much a daydream in the beginning, *so grab a pen and paper, sit somewhere quiet and start dreaming.*

Write a short summary of what you see as the Big Picture for each category below. You remember how this daydreaming, goal setting process goes – just make a list of everything you want to have, do or be. Then prioritize, and turn your dreams into goals.

First, daydream about your...

Career • Sales Volume • Income
Then prioritize and turn those #1's into goals.

To reach these goals, you need activity goals to develop your...

Skills • Work Habits • Customer Base

Hitting your result and activity goals requires continuing...

Education • Discipline • Success Attitude

To make goal setting a part of your life...

❑ Get a 3 ring binder and call it "My Goals".

❑ Create categories in all of the above areas.

❑ In each category, create a fairly specific 3 to 5-year goal.

❑ Break those 3 to 5-year goals into very specific 1-year goals.

❑ Break those goals into 6-month, 90-day, and monthly goals.

❑ Mark DONE, ✓ it off or add a happy face when you hit a goal.

❑ Don't forget to create some rewards for hitting some goals.

❑ Keep your notebooks forever. I promise, you'll be as shocked as I was, when you look back at them 30 years from now.

Examples Of Professional Goals To Set...

Status...

- Become the #1 salesperson in the dealership.
- Become the #1 salesperson in the region.
- Become the #1 salesperson in the zone.
- Become the #1 salesperson in the country.
- Become the #1 salesperson in the world.

Units...

- Raise my current average 1 unit every 90 days.
- Raise my current average to _____ by this time next year.
- Raise my current average to _____ by __ / __ (90 days from now).
- Raise my current average to _____ by __ / __ (1 year from now).
- Raise my current average to _____ 3 years from now.
- Raise my current average to _____ 5 years from now.
- Exceed the monthly sales record at my dealership of ___ by __ / __.
- Exceed the annual sales record at my dealership of ___ by __ / __.

Income...

- Earn $ _____ this month.
- Earn $ _____ this quarter.
- Earn $ _____ this year.
- Earn $ _____ in the next 3 years.
- Earn $ _____ in the next 5 years.

Customer Satisfaction...

- Have 100% Customer Satisfaction every month by ___ / ___ / ___.
- Have 100% of my business come from repeat and referral customers by ___ / ___ / ___ .

Gross...

• Raise my current average commission per unit $_____ by ___ / ___.

• Exceed my highest personal gross on a single unit of $ _____
by __ /__ /__.

• Exceed the dealership's highest gross of $ _____ on a single
unit by __ /__ /__.

• Exceed my highest total gross in a month which is $ _____
by __ /__ /__.

• Exceed the dealership's highest total gross in a single month
which is $ _____ by __ /__ /__.

Other...

• Lease _____ units per month by __ /__ /__.

• Hire someone to help me with my follow up by __ /__ /__.

• Own a __ bedroom, __ bath home with a __ car garage on __
acres, with a _____ by ___ /___ /___.

• Own a twin-engine turbo prop airplane by ___ /___ /___.

• _____ by ___ / ___ / ___.

Your Specific Selling Skills...

I will improve my following selling skills...

• _____ by ___ / ___ / ___

• _____ by ___ / ___ / ___

• _____ by ___ / ___ / ___

• _____ by ___ / ___ / ___

• _____ by ___ / ___ / ___

• _____ by ___ / ___ / ___

Selling skills should be an ongoing section in your goal book.

There are so many more worthwhile things you can do.
Just think about it - set a goal - write a plan - work your plan!

My 'Big Picture' Goals
Career – Units – Income

*Expand this goal setting page in your
'Goals Binder' for all three of the areas listed above.*

In general, I'd like to see myself... _____

_____

_____

My 3 to 5-Year Goals

In ____ years, I will... _____

_____

My 1-Year Goals

By _____ / _____ / _____, I will... _____

_____

My 6-Month Goals

By _____ / _____ / _____, I will... _____

_____

My 90-Day Goals

By _____ / _____ / _____, I will... _____

_____

Next, create your <u>activity</u> action plan for each of your goals.

One of those choices...

It's so easy to justify not making those trades to hit your goals – the extra 20 minutes to train on JVTN®, the money to attend our 3 different sales workshops, the 6 days away from the dealership, and, and, and. There are always reasons not to – but here's what most people don't consider...

Which do you prefer – $1 million, $2 million or $4 million?

Everybody reading this will earn a million dollars; that isn't even a question. The only question is: *How long it will take them?*

If you earn $50,000 / year now, that's $4,166 per month and if you keep that up, in the next 20 years, you'll earn $1,000,000 selling cars. That's an above-average income, so congratulations.

If you attend our 3 classes (6 days total), and use JVTN® to train daily to develop your skills, and go to work to work – you'll hit your $100,000 per year goal, and continue to improve year after year.

Earning $100,000 per year is $8,333 per month, which means you'll earn *at least* $2,000,000 selling cars in the next 20 years. If you choose to learn and train even more to improve even more, you can earn $4,000,000 *plus* in the same 20 years instead.

The point is – you have a choice to make. Like it or not, you're going to work every day for the next 20 years (7,300 days). So you have to choose one option right now that will affect your income and your family's lifestyle for the next 20 years. No, you can't avoid making this choice because putting off your decision simply defaults your choice to 'doing nothing different'. Time does not wait, so will you...

❑ Do nothing different, justify why you won't bother, and only earn $50,000 per year for a total of $1 million in the next 20 years?

❑ Spend just 6 of those next 7,300 days attending class, and then train daily on JVTN® to improve your skills and earn $2 or $4 million for you and your family instead?

The crummy part of reading the book "Choices" – it reminded me that *once you become aware of an option – it becomes a conscious choice.* Now if you don't say, "Yes, I will," – *you choose* – "No, I won't."

If you're still unsure whether or not it's worth it to make an extra million or two in the next few years, just go home and say...

"Honey, I just learned how I could double my income and earn an extra million or two in the next 20 years, plus I'd end up working fewer days and hours – do you think I should do it?"

CHAPTER 15

GOALS TO IMPROVE YOUR SKILLS IN SALES

To reach your unit, income, and career goals in sales, you'll need to improve your skills, your work habits, your attitude and your choice of customers.

This checklist of those skills, work habits, attitudes, and customer choices is one you'll want to revisit every month, or at the very least, every quarter.

Why? Because no matter what other goals you set, everything on these lists will either get you there faster or they can hold you back.

Some or all of these will be the foundation for almost every goal you set in sales or sales management. Please feel free to add anything else to these lists you want to review regularly.

How To Improve To Your Next Level

To move up from around 10 units now, to 15 to 20 units per month...

If you're stuck around 10 units now, the first thing you have to figure out is *why* you've settled there. Those reasons will quickly show up as you check things off on these lists.

Let me be clear, this <u>is not</u> a checklist of negatives to point out how bad you are in sales, even if you check everything. This is a list of the skills, work habits, attitudes, customer choices, and other processes that *when you improve, will help you grow.*

☞ Tip: Read through these next few pages quickly the first time so you get a feel for the statements. Then start over and *check every statement that (honestly) applies to you* so you'll know exactly what areas to work on to set clear goals so you can improve and grow.

Let's Start With You, Personally...

- ❑ I'm not really sold on being in 'sales'
- ❑ I seem to lack the motivation to try harder
- ❑ I'm a little, or somewhat uncomfortable on 'commission only'
- ❑ I'm not very organized, and waste too much of my day
- ❑ I'm fairly well-organized, but still waste too much of my day
- ❑ I don't really come to work to work, I could easily work smarter
- ❑ I'm easily distracted at work by other people or things
- ❑ I've gotten / I get trapped in the huddle too often
- ❑ I'm easily influenced by some of the other salespeople
- ❑ I'm easily intimidated by some of the other salespeople
- ❑ I'm sometimes or often intimidated by some of my prospects
- ❑ I dress the way I did in my last job, not like the pro you describe
- ❑ I have low financial needs, and don't need to make much money
- ❑ I lack confidence in myself as a salesperson
- ❑ I have low, or no real expectations of myself in sales
- ❑ I do not have clear goals on what I want to accomplish in sales

About Selling...

- ❑ I sort of do, but I don't really understand 'sales'
- ❑ I'm uncomfortable trying to 'sell' people things
- ❑ I haven't had much training on how to sell
- ❑ I'm not very comfortable around a lot of my customers
- ❑ I sometimes feel awkward and unsure of what to say
- ❑ I spend most of my day waiting for a prospect
- ❑ I pre-qualify most prospects on price to *select* a vehicle
- ❑ I pre-qualify almost everyone to determine if they *can* buy
- ❑ I really don't treat everyone as a buyer *today*
- ❑ I don't do the best job I'm capable of with each prospect
- ❑ I don't really listen very well when I'm with a prospect
- ❑ I have a hard time staying focused when I'm with a prospect
- ❑ I spend a lot of time talking price, trade, down or payments
- ❑ I need to improve my appearance to make a better 1st Impression
- ❑ I greet people with some version of, "Can I help you?"
- ❑ I don't spend much time, or enough time, building rapport
- ❑ I don't spend much time, or enough time, finding wants or needs
- ❑ I give fewer than 75% of my prospects a good demonstration
- ❑ I give presentations before, instead of as part of a demonstration
- ❑ I give fewer than 75% of my prospects a good presentation
- ❑ I don't know enough *specific* product knowledge to cover FABs
- ❑ I spend too much time just *telling* people things
- ❑ I don't control the sale very well
- ❑ I don't ask many, or enough questions to find their hot buttons
- ❑ I don't introduce my prospects to Service in my Wander Around
- ❑ I don't have an Evidence Manual, or don't use it if I have one

❏ I usually focus on price in most of my closing questions

❏ I use the worst type of closing questions (yes or no questions)

❏ I'm fearful of trying to close because I may hear, "No," and I really don't know what to say or do next

❏ I don't ask for the order at least 5 times with each prospect

❏ I don't really know what to do when I get objections

❏ I focus on price, trade, down or payments when I get objections

❏ I don't try to write-up people I don't think *can* or *will* buy

❏ I write a lot of people up who are loosely committed, if that

❏ I don't follow procedures and I take shortcuts in the write-up process

❏ I usually work my managers harder than I work my prospects

❏ I'm not very comfortable in the negotiation

❏ I'm afraid I'll lose the sale if I try to take control in the negotiation

❏ I'm not very good in the negotiation

❏ When I sell a vehicle, there are a lot of loose ends in my paperwork

❏ Other than my CSI call or letter, I don't follow-up after the sale

❏ If I don't sell the vehicle, I usually don't get their contact info

❏ If I don't sell the vehicle, I don't follow-up to get them back in

❏ I don't have a follow-up *process* in place for my unsold prospects

❏ I don't get someone else, a manager or another salesperson, involved when I can't close the sale right now, today

❏ When I do get someone else involved, I usually wait until I've burned them out and it's too late for anybody to save my deal

❏ I don't have a follow-up *process* in place for my *sold* customers

❏ I *don't follow-up* my sold prospects to generate future business

❏ I don't handle *incoming sales calls* correctly to get 90% appointments

❏ I either talk *price* or try to *educate* prospects on the phone

❏ I do not have a 'show' ratio of 60%+ on phone appointments

❏ I don't track all of my selling opportunities by type of prospect

❏ I don't track all of my selling activities – presentations, demonstrations, write-ups, outgoing prospecting calls, etc.

❑ I don't track all of my sales by type, type of prospect & total income

❑ I don't track my unit sales by my 90-day current average

❑ I don't chart and graph my units and income month to month

❑ I don't use my 90-day current average to set improvement goals

❑ I don't have clear, written, specific goals for the next 12 months

❑ I don't use the VSA®, WPG, Joe's planner each day

❑ I don't have a Master List I use to follow-up and prospect

❑ I don't contact my previous customers every 90 days by phone and every 45 days by mail or e-mail

❑ I don't send my newsletter to all of my prospects every 45 days

❑ I don't know the simple 5-question Joe Verde Referral Script

❑ I don't make 5 prospecting calls per day to my sold customers

❑ I don't make at least 5 prospecting calls per day & use the script

❑ I don't meet at least 5 Service customers every day to prospect

❑ I have not been to Joe's *core* sales skills workshop

❑ I don't train on JVTN® every day for at least 10 minutes

Even if you checked everything on these lists, that's OK.
Here's your plan to get you out of that 10 car rut right away...

1. Set your unit and income results goals for 1 year, then 6 months, and then for the next 90 days. Just break it down.

2. There are so many easy things on these lists you can improve. Some require almost no effort, so select 12 easy things on these lists you can fix right away just by creating a simple checklist in your daily work plan.

3. Select 12 bigger things you will correct within 90 days that will move you to that 15 to 20 range within 1 year. Turn each into a clear goal and create specific plans, here, too.

4. Select the 4 you will improve this month. Set your goals, create your plans, and then go to work.

5. In 90 days, review your 1-year goal, set new goals for your next 90 days, create your plans, and keep improving yourself.

You can do this!

To move from the 20, 30 or 40 unit range to your next level...

You'll notice that the list itself doesn't change as you keep moving up in levels. Even when you do master something on the list, you'll need to continually review and reinforce every skill, work habit, attitude and your choice of customers, or you'll lose it fast.

I'll explain even more after you check this list once more. Now that you're in the 20+ range, check the things you *still* need to work on.

"Still need to work on" are the key words.

About You...

❑ I'm *still* not really sold on being in 'sales'

❑ I *still* seem to lack the motivation to try harder

❑ I'm *still* a little, or somewhat uncomfortable on commission only

❑ I'm *still* not very organized and waste too much of my day

❑ I'm *still* pretty organized but still waste too much of my day

❑ I *still* don't really come to work to work ... and I'm not sure why

❑ I'm *still* easily distracted at work by other people or things

❑ I've *still* gotten trapped in the huddle

❑ I'm *still* easily influenced by the other salespeople

❑ I'm *still* easily intimidated by the other salespeople

❑ I'm *still* often intimidated by some of my prospects

❑ I *still* dress the way I always did – not like the pro you described

❑ I *still* have low financial needs and don't need much money

❑ I *still* lack quite a bit of confidence in myself as a salesperson

❑ I *still* have low expectations of myself in sales

❑ I *still* don't really have clear goals on what I want to do in sales

About Selling...

❑ I *still* don't really understand sales

❑ I'm *still* uncomfortable trying to 'sell' people things

❑ I *still* haven't had much training on how to sell

❑ I'm *still* not very comfortable around people

❑ I *still* feel awkward sometimes and unsure of what to say

❑ I *still* spend most of my day waiting for a prospect

Goal Setting

- [ ] When I get a prospect, I *still* pre-qualify almost everyone on *price*
- [ ] I *still* pre-qualify almost everyone on whether I think they *can* buy
- [ ] I *still* don't treat every prospect as a buyer today
- [ ] I *still* don't do the best job I'm capable of with each prospect
- [ ] I *still* don't really listen very well when I'm with a prospect
- [ ] I *still* have a hard time staying focused when I'm with a prospect
- [ ] I *still* spend a lot of time talking price, trade, down or payments
- [ ] I *still* need to improve my appearance to make a better 1st Impr.
- [ ] I *still* greet people with some version of, "Can I help you?"
- [ ] I *still* don't spend much time, or enough time, building rapport
- [ ] I *still* don't spend much time, or enough time, investigating
- [ ] I *still* give fewer than 75% of my prospects a good presentation
- [ ] I *still* give presentations before, instead of as part of my demo
- [ ] I *still* don't know enough specific product info to cover FABs
- [ ] I *still* spend too much time just *telling* people things
- [ ] I *still* give fewer than 75% of my prospects a good demonstration
- [ ] I *still* don't control the sale very well
- [ ] I *still* don't ask many of the questions that I've read in here
- [ ] I *still* don't introduce my prospects to Service
- [ ] I *still* don't have an Evidence Manual or don't use it if I have on
- [ ] I *still* use the worst type of closing questions you described in he
- [ ] I *still* focus on price in most of my closing questions
- [ ] I'm *still* fearful of trying to close because I may hear, "No"
- [ ] I *still* don't ask for the order at least 5 times with each prosp
- [ ] I *still* don't really know what to do when I get objections
- [ ] I *still* focus on price, trade, down and payments when I get object
- [ ] I *still* don't try to write up people who I don't think *can* or *wi*
- [ ] I *still* write people up who are very loosely committed, if a
- [ ] I *still* don't follow procedures and take shortcuts in the w

- ☐ I *still* work my managers harder than I work my prospects
- ☐ I'm *still* not very comfortable in the negotiation
- ☐ I'm *still* not very good in the negotiation
- ☐ When I sell a vehicle, there are *still* loose ends in my paperwork
- ☐ Other than my CSI call or letter, I *still* don't follow-up after the sale
- If I don't sell the vehicle, I *still* don't get the prospect's follow-up information so I can call them back
- If I don't sell the vehicle, I *still* don't follow-up to get them back in
- *still* don't get someone else, manager or salesperson, involved en I can't close the sale today
- get someone else involved, but it's *still* usually too late by then
- don't have a follow-up process in place for my sold rs and unsold prospects
- 't follow-up my sold prospects for future business
- t handle my incoming sales calls correctly to set ntments
- talk *price* or try to *educate* prospects on the phone
- hone appointments *still* do not show up
- ack all of my selling opportunities – floor traffic spect, incoming sales calls, internet leads, etc.
- k all of my selling activities – presentations, write ups, outgoing prospecting calls, etc.
- k all of my sales by type of sale, type of commission, bonus, etc.
- ck my unit sales by my 90-day average
- art and graph my units and income, month to month
- se my current average to set goals for improvement
- have clear, written and specific goals this year
- use the VSA®, WPG, Joe's planner or a daily to make sure I stay focused & on track at work

❑ I *still* don't have a Master List of my customers and prospects that I use to follow-up and prospect

❑ I *still* don't contact my previous customers every 90 days by phone and every 45 days by mail or email

❑ I *still* don't send my newsletter to all of my prospects every 45 days

❑ I *still* don't know Joe's 5-question Referral Script

❑ I *still* don't make 5 calls per day to follow-up my sold customers and I *still* don't use the referral script on each call

❑ I *still* don't make 5 calls per day to prospect for new business and I *still* don't use the referral script on each call

❑ I *still* don't meet at least 5 Service customers every day and I *still* don't use the referral script with each customer

❑ I *still* have not been to Joe's Sales Workshops

❑ I *still* don't train on JVTN® every day for at least 10 minutes

----

No, contrary to most people's initial thought, the list doesn't change just because you move up the ladder.

There are more skills to master than you possibly can – and then there's the ongoing maintenance required to keep your skills sharp.

Every skill on the list is important. In fact, improving in a single skill *alone* can move you up from 10 to 20 units and that means you will always have plenty of selling skills to work on.

Pride and ego are great, but they're both our biggest problems when it comes to improving our skills and work habits. The key to success is to be *brutally* honest in your self-appraisal so you know what to work on right away to improve.

☞ Tip: Make this entire section part of your quarterly review for setting goals. You'll always need to improve your skills and habits.

As long as you keep improving, you'll keep growing.

Getting From 20 To 30+
Here's where selling gets fun and much easier...

If you're at 20 now, you still have lots of areas you can improve. But you're already doing well in sales, so for the most part, getting to your next level depends on *refining* the skills you've already developed and building those other skills you checked, too.

No matter what level you reach, to improve even more, you'll always use these same lists as a quarterly evaluation.

If you're in the 20-30+ range now – you like sales, you go to work to work, you can definitely sell, you're reasonably organized, you either follow-up and prospect or *some* customers like you enough to come back in to see you anyway, and you either *have the goal to succeed* or you *need the money* that goes with being a high achiever.

At your level of sales, it's time to start focusing on *specific areas* that will make you more effective and build your business, so you can sell more vehicles every month.

✓ **Organizational skills are HUGE now.**

You have to learn how to control your day, so you can get more done. To save time, you need a *follow-up system* instead of just doing follow-up. You need a *prospecting system* and you need a *process* to automatically remind you of who to call, why you're calling and to keep that 45 / 90-day follow-up going for you.

Tip: Start using the Virtual Sales Assistant® (VSA®). I designed it *just for salespeople* to control their customer base, set goals, and track their selling activities and results. It's on JVTN®, which means you most likely already have it, so start using it now!

✓ **At the 20 to 30+ level, tracking everything you do is critical.**

At your level, you need to *refine* your skills even more. To do that you have to know *exactly* what to work on. That's why you have to track every opportunity, activity and result you get in sales. Start using the VSA® to track everything you do. It will take care of your averages, projections and your charts.

No time to track? That's no excuse! With our planners or the VSA®, it will take you less than 2 minutes per day to keep up with everything you're doing in sales. That is, unless you sell something – then it will take you 3 or 4 minutes each day.

✓ **You need clear and specific daily goals.**

You have to focus on your priorities each day (the steps to your longer term goals). That means you have to learn how to set goals in every area that is important in sales. You understand those now, because that's what this entire book has been about.

✓ **Master the phone.**

All high achievers know the telephone is their secret to success in sales. If you know how to use it, that's great and now it's time to master every type of call. The telephone is your most important tool in sales to help you sell more *today* and to build a solid customer base. Get to our Business Development Workshop and go through the Business Development courses on JVTN®.

✓ **Stay focused on your critical tasks.**

We've talked about 'Traps' and mistakes. Well, one of the biggest mistakes high achievers make is that they start skipping steps, especially demos and follow-up, when they're busy. And from what you've learned in the stats, now you know that skipping demos costs you sales *today* – and skipping your follow-up costs you sales *tomorrow*. You can't grow if you keep missing those easy sales so again, organization is critical.

Tip: Get help! There will be a point when you need an assistant or someone to help you with some of the *stuff* so you can be more productive and sell more units.

A helper can make calls, schedule appointments, do follow-up, help with paperwork when you're with more than one customer, take a customer to Service for you, and just about anything else to help free up your time so you can do what you do best (and what you get paid to do) – *sell more cars!*

Yes, you can hope your dealer will help you because if you're stuck in that "time/space" continuum, you and the dealership are losing sales simply because you're out of time. Mine wouldn't help me, and if yours won't help you, there are two choices; get mad, simmer and lose sales or hire someone yourself. A part time student, your (mature) kids, parents who want to work from home, etc. can help you and don't have to cost a lot.

✓ **More effective closing and objection handling skills.**

You can't just do you best and hope people buy. Closing is part of selling and most sales have to be closed or you'll miss too many of them. We have workshops on Selling, and on Closing and Negotiating. Get to class and take those courses on JVTN® now.

✓ **Improved negotiation skills.**

Even high achievers too often jump to price when they're busy because it *seems* faster. No matter why you justify it, focusing on price costs you sales and gross on every delivery you make.

Better selling and closing skills make negotiations easier, and having more effective negotiation skills and especially keeping the negotiation away from price and on *budget* is the key to closing more of the deals you're writing now.

Same thing – get to our Closing and Negotiation Workshop right away. All of our classes (processes) on selling, closing and negotiation, and our courses on JVTN® work together to help you deliver more units, in less time, with higher gross profits.

✓ **Get better at avoiding all "price" talk on the lot.**

Learn how to bypass every question, concern and objection that has to do with price and stop talking price on the lot, period. Go through the PRICE course and the Closing on Objections courses on JVTN®.

✓ **Stop working bell-to-bell every day.**

Do work a ton in the beginning of your career to get good or when you're at your new dealership to establish yourself, and then switch to working *smart.* In the end, 70 and 80-hour work weeks just wear you down and cost you sales and income.

Tip: Find a partner in sales like I did with my friend, Paul. We were both 30-car guys, and split deals almost every day. Having a partner *who can sell,* that you can trust who also works on the opposite shift, really helps you have a life outside the dealership and helps you make money even when you aren't at work.

Half of something is always better than all of nothing.

✓ **Make a commitment to constantly improve everything you do each quarter and each year, *without exception.***

Put an automatic goal setting process in place or a reminder in your calendar to remind you every 30 to 90 days to set new improvement goals for both your *results* and your *activities.*

I'm sure you remember by now to always set your activity and result goals based on your current average in each area (your most recent rolling 90-day average). Just don't sell so many units that you forget to keep setting goals.

As long as you keep setting goals to improve, and as long as you keep working on your skills, your work habits and focusing on your best customers, you'll automatically retain that great attitude pros in sales must have to keep growing.

At these levels, you're a professional and you're doing great. Now to keep moving your current average higher, just track everything you do, set a goal to improve, write your plan of action and then just work your plan every single day!

Congratulations – You're A Sales Professional!

"Listen to the whispers of your mind.
They're telling you the choices that will help you the most."

– Choices

"14 to 25 after JVTN®"

"Joe, I have been selling cars for 10 years. My first 8 years I was up to a 14 car average and was making about $40,000. Not bad, but I wanted more so I started training on JVTN® my ninth year.

I began implementing the process and recently had my biggest month ever and set a store record with 34 units! My current average is 25 now and I am on track for $100,000 for this year!

The best part is I am still learning and growing daily as I continue my training on JVTN®. Thanks for a great process that works and is helping me get to the next level!"

— Toyota Salesperson, Milwaukee, WI

"From 14 to 22 units with JVTN®"

"I've sold cars for 6 years now and was averaging 14 units a month. My dealership got Joe Verde's Online Training® and Joe's book, 'How to Sell a Car Today'.

For one month I trained, practiced and applied what I learned out on the lot daily and sold 22 units. I have had other sales training and I must say, nothing comes close to the Joe Verde way!"

— Keith, Salesperson, Hyundai, ON, Canada

"From $60,000 per year to $112,000 with Joe Verde Training"

"I was averaging $60,000 per year before I attended my first Joe Verde Workshop 5 years ago, and I have attended 4 more since then: the 2 Day Sales Workshop (twice), Closing and Negotiating Workshop, and most recently the Phone and Internet Workshop.

I sell the Joe Verde way, focusing on the customer's wants and needs. Not creating objections, but handling them and now I am averaging $112,000 per year and love my profession!"

— Ford Salesperson, Brandon, MB, Canada

SPECIAL SECTION

This Special Section has been edited and reprinted by permission of Joe Verde from his book, "Earn Over $100,000 Selling Cars Every Year".

You can download a PDF or order a printed copy at...

www.joeverde.com/store

CHAPTER 16

SHORTCUTS TO SKILL DEVELOPMENT

There's no shortcut to success or to the sale, but I'll show you how to take the only shortcut there is in selling, and that's developing your skills *faster,* so you can start closing more sales *sooner.*

First, let's look at the four stages of developing your skills in anything you do. And then I'll give you several tips on how you can learn *more,* and learn it *faster.*

There are 4 stages of skill development…

1. Unconsciously Incompetent.

> Example: In Boxing: I keep getting knocked out and I have no idea how to fight back or defend myself.

I'm not any good and I have no idea why.

This means exactly what it says – people at this level don't even know what they don't know. These people aren't very good at their jobs – they can't be because they don't know anything.

In fact, this pretty much describes my own skill level during my first five years. I certainly knew *some* things about a car just from owning them, but because we didn't get any training on how to follow the Basics, or on how to close the sale, overcome objections, or negotiate, I couldn't actually *sell* – and I didn't know why.

I couldn't follow-up my unsold prospects to pick up those other 8 sales most 10-car guys miss, because I didn't even know why I should follow-up, much less how to follow-up. As for my phone skills, I had no idea what I was supposed to do, so I missed all of those opportunities, too.

Because picking up just those 8 sales apiece from unsold follow-up would have doubled my sales at my first dealership – I can only assume my manager wasn't trained and didn't know how to teach us how to follow-up, either.

Check the key skills you really don't understand at all...

❏ Warm Up: 1st Impressions, Greeting, Rapport, Investigation
❏ Value Building: Sell Service, Evidence, Presentation, Demo
❏ Closing: Summary Close, Assumptive, Action, Final Close
❏ Objections: Bypass, Clarify, Rephrase, Isolate, Close, Refocus
❏ Negotiate: Set Up, 1st Pass, 2nd Pass Gross, 3rd Pass Wrap Up
❏ Sales Calls: Control, Expand Inventory, Appointment, Anchor
❏ Internet Leads: 1st Reply, The $, The Call, Appt., Anchor
❏ Unsold Follow-Up: T/U Note, 1st, 2nd, 3rd Call, Your System
❏ Retention: Delivery, 1st Service, 6-Step F/Up, Retention Process

2. Consciously Incompetent.

> Example: In Boxing: I'm still getting knocked out, but now I
> know what I need to do to win.

I'm still not any good, but now I know what I don't know.

Once I started reading books on selling, the 'ah, that makes sense' lights started coming on. And the more I read, the more I realized there were skills in sales I had never even thought of that would help me sell more cars, have more fun and make more money.

I didn't have the skills, but I learned what they were.

The good news is that by being *aware* of things I didn't know, it also made me *aware of the benefits* to me of developing these new skills.

Most people are serious about selling more, and becoming aware of what we don't know is generally all it takes to motivate most people to really dig in and learn how to grow and improve. In fact, who wouldn't want to develop the skills they know would help them sell more, earn more and provide more for themselves and their family?

If you've been reading this book with an open mind, you have reached this 2nd level on the skills you didn't realize that you needed to improve. Now the real work starts...

Write down the 5 most important skills you know you need and why.

1. _____

  Why? _____

2. _____

  Why? _____

3. _____

  Why? _____

4. _____

  Why? _____

5. _____

  Why? _____

3. Consciously Competent.

Example: In Boxing: My boxing skills are improving, but I'm still not responding fast enough and I have to think about what to do. I'm still hitting the canvas now and then, but I'm winning more fights than ever.

I am getting better, but I still have to consciously think too much about how to do what I've been learning.

At this level, I was learning the skills I needed in sales, but using them was still hard work because I had to really focus on everything I was saying and doing.

Because I hadn't mastered the skills yet, selling was a mental chess game as I tried to remember what I was supposed to be saying and doing each step along the way.

Even though I was selling more at this level, now I was even more aware of the sales I was missing. Why? Because now I could replay the sale in my mind, and I could spot exactly where and why I didn't make each sale I missed.

What skills are you using that are working for you now – but that you know you need to improve even more?

- _____
- _____
- _____
- _____
- _____
- _____
- _____
- _____
- _____
- _____
- _____
- _____

4. Unconsciously Competent.

Example: In Boxing: I'm good, I fight instinctively now and I
am winning almost every time.

Selling is now a no-brainer and doesn't require conscious thought!

Underline the key skills in the next paragraph you've mastered, and
then go back and highlight the ones that still need improvement...

Now you can turn internet leads into calls and into appointments
that show, answer incoming calls correctly, bypass price, and turn
them into appointments that show, get names & numbers so you can
follow-up the people who don't buy, make that first follow-up call,
avoid price, close on the appointment, anchor it and have them show
on the lot, prospect by phone with the 5-question referral script,
work the Service Drive for referrals, and when you get a customer
on the lot – greet them, make a great 1st impression, bypass price,
control the conversation and process, build rapport, find their hot
buttons, sell Service and the dealership, answer their questions, select
the vehicle you'll send them home in, drive first on the demo to cover
FABs they care most about, give the secondary buyer a great targeted
presentation & demo, give the primary buyer a great targeted
presentation & demo, start your closing sequence at the landmark,
use your assumptive close as you pull on the lot, get a dozen action
closes, finish it off with your final closing question, clarify, rephrase,
isolate and close again on objections they bring up, set up the
negotiation properly, start it with that 1st-pass to pull their highest
KTB numbers, 2nd-pass to go for the gross and the 3rd-pass to wrap
it up and get a bump, complete all of the paperwork, transition it
correctly to Finance, make their first Service appointment before they
take delivery, deliver it properly, start the 6-step follow-up process
for sold customers with a thank you note, first call, 'who's who',
duplicate 'who's who', mailing list, master list, 45-day mailouts,
90-day calls and then working with the rest of the dealership team,
complete the retention process – so you can start it all over again,
and of course, follow up every prospect you don't sell.

*The Catch...*after you've mastered any skill – just like the professional
boxer in these examples, you have to keep practicing everything daily
to retain your new skills so you can keep winning year after year.

How To Develop Your Skills Faster

There's a slow route and a faster route to developing skills. If you were to take the slow route, you could spend several years developing the basic skills it takes to turn 'pro' in sales.

Or you can take these shortcuts and spend a few days to work on some of the easier skills, a few weeks for the mid-range skills and a few months to really hone the major skills until you've mastered them. These will be the skills you get to keep forever (with maintenance).

The following are the quick and easy shortcuts you can follow that will save you years of frustration and years of lost sales.

Slow down...

When you read my books, attend our workshops or go through chapters on JVTN®, remember the goal is to learn more, not to see how fast you can get through the material. We have some people who pride themselves on having watched 500 chapters on JVTN®.

I used the word 'watched' 500 chapters instead of 'taken' because you can't *properly* go through an 8-minute online training chapter in just 8 minutes and internalize the skill. Don't confuse quantity with quality, because when you're trying to develop selling skills – *speed kills*.

Retention...

You've forgotten 60% of what you read or heard just 20 minutes ago and by tomorrow, it's closer to 90% unless you work hard to retain it.

Example: Don't look up these stats, just answer these questions...

1. What % of the prospects who leave without buying will return with good follow-up? ___% What % will buy when they come back? ___% Understanding and doing unsold follow-up daily can just about double your sales and income.

2. What % of the features on your vehicles do your customers really care about? ___% (That's why you find their hot buttons.)

3. What % will shop price if you give it to them on the lot, on the phone or in email? ___% (That's why you learn to bypass.)

See what I mean by speed reading?
The goal is to learn, not to go fast!

We learn through repetition.

If you hear or read something 6 times, you'll remember 50% of it. You'll remember even more *and be able to use* what you learn, if you put in some extra effort to develop your skills.

Don't just read or watch a training chapter on JVTN® – develop your skills.

Reading a book or watching a video won't change your income, *applying* what you learn is the only way to do that. Your goal is to take the information you learn and turn it into a skill that you own. Developing skills takes practice, practice, and more practice.

Some quick tips on developing your skills...

1. **Prepare yourself to retain more of what you learn.**

   Never start reading a book or start training on JVTN® without a pen, paper and a highlighter, so you can take great notes.

   Remember, you forget almost everything you hear, except what you highlight, write down and then review later.

   If you haven't done this already, go get a 3-ring binder for your training, and add notes on everything you learn, starting today. This will become your personal training manual.

   Create three main sections called: Get, Sell, and Keep.

   • **Get:** This section will include your Unsold Follow-Up, Prospecting, Sales Calls, Internet Leads, using Social Media.

   • **Sell:** This section will include all of the skills in The New Basics™, Handling Price & Objections, Closing, Negotiation.

   • **Keep:** Include everything you learn about retaining customers: Sold Follow-Up, Retention Skills & Processes.

   All of our classes come with complete workbooks and homework books, and you can print all of the workbooks and homework for the courses on JVTN®. Add those to your 3-ring binder, so you have everything in one place for easy reference.

   As you start learning more, your first binder will get too big and soon each section will need its own 3-ring binder. And every time you add pages and sections from what you're learning, your sales grow and your paychecks get bigger.

2. **Go through a JVTN® course the first time to get the big picture.
Then go through it as many times as it takes to develop your skills.**

Example: "How To Sell More Cars Every Month" (the selling
process). It's 22 chapters, and about 3 hours in length.

How fast could you watch it? That's just math – you could watch
the entire series before noon, and even take a few breaks. And
that's OK, if you're just viewing it the first time to understand the
big picture, before you start developing your skills.

How fast should you go through the course though, to *develop*
your skills? *That's a different story.*

Completing this course *correctly* should take you at least a month.
If you go through the whole course in the first few days just to get
the big picture, again that's fine, but that's just to get an overview.

After that overview though, you need to slow down and spend
30 to 45 days reviewing key chapters and key skills, again and
again until you master each skill. Then when you've *completed*
this course, you'll have developed solid skills that will take your
selling and income average to a new and higher level right away.
To stay at that new level, make sure you review all of the core
JVTN® training courses at least twice each year.

Tip: Pause after each chapter to 'think it over' a little.

There are more than a dozen *core skills courses* in JVTN® that
you have to develop, and then there are a ton of other courses,
and another few hundred specific topics, too. Take your time to
really understand and learn everything we cover.

It's important to slow down, because every BIG skill is made up
of a lot of smaller skills. Like a book, each chapter in a course
on JVTN® builds on the previous chapter and adds skills as it
progresses. That means it's critical that you understand each
point before you move to the next chapter.

Speed Kills!

*Your goal is to develop skills, so slow down and
stick with one course until you master those specific skills.*

3. Wear out your books & workbooks from class & JVTN®.

I have two kinds of books on my shelf – the ones in great shape because they weren't very good, so I only read through them once and the ones I've worn out from reading again and again and from taking notes and marking up the pages.

Really use your workbooks and homework books from class to help you develop skills. They aren't meant to sit on a shelf. They're filled with skills, processes, activities and scripts on everything we cover in class *and then some*. They won't make you a penny sitting on the shelf or stuck in a box somewhere.

Same thing with all of the sales courses you have on JVTN®. In fact, because we add new chapters and new games or role plays and mini-series all the time, it's highly unlikely you'll ever even complete all the training, the games and role plays that are on JVTN®, no matter how hard you try.

Our JVTN® courses cover complete processes. Most chapters in a course are in the 6-10 minute range, which is perfect for training on a time budget. Plus, if you have a smartphone, you can even train on JVTN® while you're waiting for your next appointment to show up. You can also access the VSA® on your smartphone to add your tracking and customer information.

Treat JVTN® and all of our courses as a *technical manual on selling*. Pick a skill each month to focus on, then learn something about that topic every day – use my books, your workbooks, or the chapters on JVTN®.

Tag your *favorites* as you go through JVTN® chapters so you can easily find them again. Use the *key word search* to help you find a topic quick when you need it.

For example, if you have an important call to make, use the *search* feature to find 'Sales Calls' and review 'Getting Ready To Pick Up The Phone' or review the call scripts in the VSA® so you're prepared and ready to take control of the call.

Highlight important points, dog-ear your favorite pages in the books, put sticky notes on pages to review, go through a chapter on JVTN® with breakfast – just learn something every day!

4. Practice, practice, practice!

There's no shortcut to turn what you learn into skills you can use. Developing skills requires a clear goal on what you want to accomplish (learn), a clear and specific plan you can follow and it takes practice and more practice to develop your skills.

Note: Reading something 10 times isn't practice, that's reading it 10 times. Saying the words out loud is only part of practicing. Focusing on your tone and inflection and delivery is part of practice. Having someone role play with you is also part of practicing.

5. Evaluate and chart your skill level!

After you've taken or read a chapter, and after you've reviewed your notes, evaluate yourself on that topic every 30 to 60 days. Use a 1–10 rating and chart your numbers. Why? Because when you're focusing on a skill, your ratings will go up. When you stop focusing on a skill, they'll likely drop. A consistent rating schedule will help keep your skills in tip-top shape.

6. Focus on your potential so that you stay pumped!

In your notes, rate your potential for improvement. How many more units could you see yourself selling this month *if* you improved your skills, or improved your habits or your attitude in those skills, habits, attitude and customer choice questions?

You'll be shocked at how quickly your sales potential builds as you learn more. Be realistic – don't highball yourself. Start here and fill in these three guesstimates...

1. How many more units would you sell if you improved, and gave every person a better demonstration? ___ units.

2. How many more units would you sell right now if you did your follow-up with every unsold prospect? ___ units.

3. How many more units would you sell right now if you knew more ways to close the sale? ___ units.

Make a commitment to learn more and let's make this the first day of your brand new career in sales!

CHAPTER 17

A DOZEN FACTS YOU NEED TO KNOW TO HELP YOU HIT YOUR GOALS FASTER

You're reading this book to learn how to set goals to improve your sales, your income and many other areas.

If you were in Las Vegas with a goal to win, and saw two tables with the same game, but one offered a 10% chance of winning and the other offered 50% or higher, *which table would you play?*

Of course, any logical person who knew the odds, would play the best odds of winning, especially when the game is the same. *And that's your edge in goal setting, too.*

There are so many statistics that point you to that "winning table" in sales, just take the guesswork out of selling more and earning more by understanding these statistics and start playing your best odds, every time.

The Quick Facts: A Baker's Dozen

About your prospects...

1. **99% of the people want to drive the vehicle before they buy it.**

    Skipping the demo is one of the costliest mistakes salespeople make and it's one of the first shortcuts most salespeople *hope* to be able to take when they're trying to sell their product.

    Why is it a mistake? The 99% stat itself says it all, so read it again – people want to drive it *before* they buy it. Why try to win by skipping a demo and having just a 1% chance of making the sale, when there's a 99% chance you'll lose?

    More important – when people are driving, they hit the highest emotional point in the sale and are taking mental ownership of your product. To you, that means the final lap of the demonstration is when you want to close the sale.

    Your Goal: Give 75% of your prospects a demo.

2. **78% of the people who go out and look at a vehicle – buy one.**

    That little dot at the end of that sentence is a *period*. That means this statistic is not open for debate and you can forget what the huddle says about this stat being incorrect.

    Even better news, these are Hot Prospects because...

    • 38% buy within 4 hours of stopping at the first dealership

    • 57% buy within 3 days

    • 90% buy within a week

    So if you're looking for a sale, don't worry about which person on the lot is a buyer, because there's an 8 out of 10 chance the one you're with will buy and there's a 50/50 chance they'll buy from you today, if you do your job right.

    Your Goal: Treat everyone as a buyer <u>now</u>.

3. **85% decided to buy a vehicle before they ever left home.**

    They really aren't 'just looking' – they say that out of habit, just like you do when a salesperson walks up to you.

    Your Goal: Stop guessing and assume they're buying.

4. **58% buy the same product they went to look at first.**

    If 78% will buy, and if 85% decided to buy a vehicle before they even left home, if you sell Fords and they show up at your Ford store first…I think it's pretty safe to say that they're not only considering buying a Ford, but they're also willing to buy it from your dealership and from you today, if you'll just take the time to do your job right.

    Your Goal: Assume they came to see you today to buy now.

5. **71% buy because they like you, trust you and respect you.**

    Ben Franklin and Socrates both talked about how important the relationship (rapport) is between the salesperson and the buyer. It was true then and it's true now, because you and I react the exact same way. If people like you, you'll have a better chance of making the sale. If they don't like you – again, good luck because you'll need it.

    Your Goal: Learn to ask questions to build rapport fast.

6. **90+% of the decisions to purchase will be influenced by the woman in the group (or at home). Plus, over 50% of the vehicles delivered, are delivered to women.**

    Quick Check: If you're a guy and if you really aren't sure how much women influence the decisions we (men) make, just go ask your wife or girlfriend or your mom or your sister.

    Your Goal: Do the job you're supposed to be doing with every person on the lot (man, woman or kid on a bicycle). You'll definitely increase your sales overnight to women, but you'll also increase your sales overall to everyone.

7. **30% of the people have a *family member* who will be buying a new or used vehicle within the next 90 days. And 62% *know someone* who will be buying within 90 days.**

   Here's a 'get rich quick' method that works like a charm and it's like pulling teeth to get salespeople to do it. It's called prospecting and follow-up and it needs to be a part of your *activity plan* every day for your sales and income goals.

   We can show you how to double sales and keep your income growing forever by developing your 'Business Development' skills: Follow-Up, Prospecting, Referral Prospecting, Building Your Master List and improving your Phone Skills.

   These skills help you sell more vehicles today, and help you keep building your business, year after year.

   Your Goal: Get to our classes, train daily on JVTN®
   and make prospecting a part of your daily activity plan!

   ### Stop Here!

   1. Go back through these first 7 stats and circle the ones you know you really need to improve right away to sell more.

   2. Set a goal to improve in that area and date it.

   3. Write a quick activity action plan to improve in that area.

"After selling for 19 years,
I doubled my sales using JVTN®."

"After 19 years I was still only at 7 or 8 cars, but in the past year I've committed to training daily on JVTN®.

I've learned to build value and stay off price, which increased my gross 25%. I have also just doubled my previous unit average that I held for 19 years in the business! What a difference!"

– SK, Salesperson, Louisiana

**Now let's look at some of the facts
about their buying motives and decisions...**

8.   **20% of the features on your vehicle – that's all your prospects
really care about, *not* everything you know about your product.**

Every prospect has Hot Buttons, and those are their own
personal reasons they want a particular product. That also
means they have Cold Buttons, and those are the things they
just don't care very much about.

If their Hot Button is Comfort and Convenience and you
spend your presentation talking about their Cold Buttons,
Performance and Economy, you're dead in the water.

Tip: Don't confuse, "We want a loaded Tahoe," with a Hot
Button – that's just what they want. It's *why* they want it
that matters most, and that comes down to specific features
and *why* they want them. Tahoe: Big and comfortable. Hot
Buttons: 4 kids, bad back, river trips, room for soccer gear.

Your Goal: Find their really 'hot' Hot Buttons.

9.   **80% of the buying (and selling) is done in your 3 presentation
steps of the sale.**

When they only care about 20% of the features on your
vehicle, after you *investigate* (find out who, how, what and
why), you have your demonstration and presentation to turn
up the heat and really light up their Hot Buttons.

To do that, your demonstration and presentation need to focus
on the *targeted* features they care about. Cover why they said they
wanted it and cover the benefits (Hot Buttons) to them of having
each and every one of those features.

*Your Goal: Find every person's Hot Buttons and light up those
features, advantages and benefits in your targeted presentation.*

10. **50% of the people buy on the spot when they get what they feel is a <u>good</u> presentation and a <u>good</u> demonstration of the product.**

    Remember that 2 or 3-car day you had awhile ago? Remember how much fun you were having and how easy you made it for your prospects to have fun, too?

    Statistically, since 78% will be buying, if you only talked to 38 people this month, 30 are buyers. Since you could close 50% of those 30 buyers – that means you could deliver 15 of the 38 people you talk to, if you'll just treat every prospect like a buyer.

    Your Goal: With every prospect... No pre-qualifying, just great rapport and investigation, killer targeted presentations, well-planned demos that build emotions, and solid closes and objection handling methods to wrap it all up.

11. **86% of the people buy a different make or model, or a different color or with different features, than they planned to purchase.**

    Hardly anybody (only 14%) drives away in *exactly what they said* they wanted. No, not because we switched them to something they didn't like. They switch because they cruise the internet, their friends show them their cars, and they think they want that white car with a sunroof and 22" wheels.

    But a lot of things happen once they're around all those other *choices* on your lot, and even more things happen when it gets down to the money it takes to buy that perfect vehicle.

    I want white, do you have one?

    • To lose the sale, respond with: "No, but I can get you one."

    • To make a sale, respond with: "Let's go see, (bypass color) who's the lucky one Bob, is the new car for you or Betty?" (As you start walking toward the lot).

    Your Goal: Expand your inventory and give everyone a chance to make a different decision by using, "Let's go see," every time you're asked about a vehicle.

12. **96% of the people who are given figures on the lot or in the office and who leave without buying – shop those figures. It's the same percentage with prices on the phone and internet.**

No matter what you've experienced or been told by the smartest 6-car guy, or *conditioned* to believe by getting beaten up over price so often – price is *not* their #1 Hot Button.

Price is #16 on people's list of buying motives, you've just forgotten to really listen to those other 15 things they say...

"We want white with a sunroof, we need third row seating for the kids, we live in the desert and need rear air, we also want the cold weather package, leather, 2nd row buckets, navigation, tow package, power tailgate, rear entertainment, roof rack, brush guard, side rails, 22" wheels and we want your best price."

Price is important to them, but you can bet that they aren't going to leave a couple of the kids at home, just because you have a 5-passenger vehicle that's cheaper.

Your Goal: Learn to listen to everything they say
so you can find their real Hot Buttons – because it isn't price.

13. **33% of the people who leave a dealership without buying will come back in with good follow-up, and when they do, 67% buy.**

It's too bad we aren't forced to follow-up with everyone, because 33% (1 out of 3) would come back with good follow-up, and 67% of them (7 out of 10) buy the vehicle on that second visit.

Do the math. If you sell 10 units now (deliver 20%) and don't follow up, if you set a goal to develop your follow up skills, and then get 75% contact info and do your follow up, you'll sell 17 cars a month instead. No extra hours, just a few phone calls.

Your Goal: 75% contact info, then make your first contact
(text, email, phone) within minutes of them leaving.

Now do the same thing you did after #7 – circle the stats you can improve, set a goal, write your plan and get to work.

Your Goal – Become A Believer!

1. 99% of the people want to drive the vehicle before they buy it.

2. 78% of the people who actually take the time to go out and look at a new or used vehicle, end up buying one (soon).

3. 85% of the people who do end up buying, decided to buy before they ever left home – we just helped them.

4. 58% of the people buy the same product they looked at first.

5. 71% of the people bought because they liked, trusted and respected the salesperson they dealt with.

6. 90%+ of the decision to purchase will be influenced by the woman in the group (or at home), and over 50% of the vehicles delivered, are purchased by women.

7. 30% of all the people have a family member who will be trading vehicles within the next 90 days, and 62% of all people know someone who will be trading within 90 days.

8. 20% of the features on your vehicles are all your prospects care about, not everything you know about your product.

9. 80% of the selling (and buying) is done in your presentation steps of the sale.

10. 50% of the people buy on the spot when they get what they feel is a good presentation and good demonstration of the product.

11. 86% of the people buy a different make or model, or a different color or with different features than they planned to purchase.

12. 96% of the people who are given figures on the lot or in the office, and who leave without buying, shop those figures, and it's the same percentage on the phones and internet.

13. 90% of the people who leave without buying are never contacted again. That's too bad because with good follow-up, 33% will come back in and 67% will buy.

You have our permission to copy this page so you can carry it with you and read it several times every day. For how long? Just until you see every person you talk to on the lot as an opportunity to make a sale on the spot, *if you do your job right.*

One Last Thing: We're back to W. I. I. F. M.
Do some quick math on what improving means to you.

1. How many units did you sell last year? $ _____

2. How much money did you earn last year? $ _____

3. Do the math on the first two; what was
    your average earnings per unit? $ _____

4. How many more units do you think you can
    sell this year if you learn more about selling
    and then set clear goals to improve?   _____ more

5. If you learn more and set clear goals, how
    much could you earn per unit? Per Unit: $ _____

Now just add up your potential...

Area						Improvement
Extra Units This Yr.	#_____	x Avg. $ Per Unit	=			$ _____
Extra Comm. Per Unit	$_____	x Total Units		=		$ _____
How much extra Bonus money would you earn?						$ _____

Total Additional Income Per Year $ _____

If you can see it, and believe it, you can do it!
Find your current averages in every area, start setting goals for
improvement and then...watch your income G R O W!

> *"From 8 to 38.5!"*
>
> *"When I first started selling cars my average was 8 per month. In the last two years I have attended two Joe Verde Workshops, I use his Monthly Planning Guide daily and his VSA® to manage my customers.*
>
> *Now my 90-day average is 38.5!*
>
> *I do well because I eat, live and breathe Joe Verde methods, training and processes. I am proof it works and I can honestly say I do not know where I would be without Joe!"*
>
> *— Trent, Salesperson, Utah*

"Luck is what happens when preparation meets opportunity."

— Elmer Letterman

Last Word...

Like I've said throughout, result and activity goal setting is your key to success. When I was learning to sell and set goals from those business leaders in different professions though, my challenge was trying to figure out how to turn what they were teaching me into goals I could set and achieve selling cars.

They taught me how to sell and how to set goals, but the one missing piece that none of them taught me was how to manage my current averages, so I could actually force growth in my units and income. That was one of the most critical and toughest problems I ran into. I knew I had to solve that problem so I could control my success and growth in sales. Once I learned to manage my *current averages*, I was able to almost completely control my sales and income every year.

These key skills are just as critical for you, too. Understanding and applying them gives you a tremendous advantage over your competition who is out there just winging it every day with poor skills, poor work habits, an average attitude (at best), and zero real goals.

Dealers, managers and salespeople in my classes over the years have used this exact process to turn a bad career around, and to turn a great career into one for the record books. That means if you'll just follow these steps, all of this will work for you, too. Just set your goals, make those plans and follow them to the end.

I'd wish you luck in your career, but luck isn't required when you have clear goals and make those commitments. Instead I'll wish you my best always, and look forward to meeting you.

Have a great career!

New Sales Tools
From Joe

More Ideas On Goal Setting!

Get more ideas and techniques from Joe
on how to set your goals, make a plan and
achieve your sales and income goals.*

Go To: www.JoeVerde.com/gs

We Want To Hear Your Results!

Goal setting is your key to success.
Tell Joe about your income & result goals
through our special comment page.

www.JoeVerde.com/comments

Get Text Messages From Joe!

Personal coaching from Joe every week
to keep you on track & make more money!

Sign Up Now!

FREE text messages from
Joe straight to your cell phone!**

Text JVTEXT To 86677

*All special offers are subject to change without notice.
**The Joe Verde Group does not charge for the service, but message and data rates may apply.
Contact your carrier for more details. Text message program available to residents of the U.S. only.

Questions? (800) 445-6217 • (949) 489-3780

Free Training
From Joe

- **Texts From Joe**
  Connect now! You'll sell more cars when you get your weekly text
  messages from Joe. Sign up online or text JVTEXT to 86677.

- **Joe Verde Blog**
  Check out the latest selling strategies to help you sell more cars at
  Joe's blog – joeverde.com/blog.

- **"Go To Work To Work" – MP3**
  Double your sales this month! Get Joe's "Go To Work To Work"
  audio file at joeverde.com and Joe will show you how.

- **Sample Joe Verde Planners**
  Get samples of Joe's planners so you can better manage your
  day, your week, your month and this year! At joeverde.com/store.

- **Joe's Sales & Manager Newsletters**
  Joe's articles about selling in today's market will prepare you for
  your next customer. Order samples online at joeverde.com/store.

- **Joe's Sales Book, "Earn Over $100K Selling Cars"**
  The secrets to success in sales are in this book. Get your printed
  copy or download the book at joeverde.com today!

- **Joe's Book For Dealers & Managers, "Recovery & Growth"**
  Follow the steps in this book and you will double or triple your net
  profit this year. Order online at joeverde.com now.

- **"Members Only" on Joe's Website**
  Sign up for our Members Only section on joeverde.com and get
  free articles, MP3 files and videos from Joe every month.

- **72-Hour Demo – JVTN®**
  Improve your selling skills and you'll improve your sales. Take
  a JVTN® test drive at www.jvtn.com.

- **30-Day Demo – Virtual Sales Assistant® (VSA®)**
  Just for salespeople: Joe's online Mini-CRM is the easy
  way for you to manage your sales & stay organized.
  Free demo at www.jvtn.com/vsa.

Questions? (800) 445-6217 • (949) 489-3780

Joe Verde Workshops
Across North America

Take charge of your career and
earn over $100,000 every year.

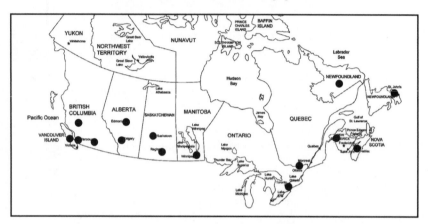

Sign Up For Class Now – Call: 800-445-6217

Questions? (800) 445-6217 • (949) 489-3780

Joe Verde Sales Training Workshops

"I sold 5 cars my first day after your class."

"Joe, I was averaging 10 cars a month, went to your class and then everything came together – I sold 5 cars and earned $4,204 my first day back at work. That's what I would normally make in a month." – Tim, Ford Salesperson, Canada

2-Day Professional Selling Skills Workshop

How To Sell A Car And Close The Sale Today!

We'll show you how to handle the changes with today's new customers so you can sell more cars right away.

2-Day Closing & Negotiating Interactive Workshop

Closing & Negotiating Are Your Keys To Success!

Learn how to present, close and overcome objections so that you can increase your gross and unit sales.

2-Day Business Development Workshop

Turn Your Phone And Internet Leads Into Deliveries Now!

Turn more of your incoming leads into appointments that show up and buy a car. We'll show you how to prospect and follow-up too, so you can also pick up some easy sales.

Sign Up And Call Today!

Questions? (800) 445-6217 • (949) 489-3780

Beware of the imposter who will promise
they can teach you everything I've just covered.

Don't waste your time and save your money.
If they really could, they would have written this book.

– Joe Verde